<
Com

1800 East County Road 42
Burnsville, MN 55337
952-432-4286

Let Me Tell You a Story

By Mervin E. Thompson

PRINCE OF PEACE PUBLISHING
Burnsville, Minnesota 55337

Library of Congress Catalog Card Number

Thompson, Mervin E., 1941
Let Me Tell You A Story

Bibliography: p.
1. Jesus Christ--Parables I. Title.
BT375.2.T54 1986 226:806 86-25-365
ISBN 0-933173-075

Printed in the United States of America

To the people of Prince of Peace Church, Burnsville, Minnesota. This book arises from our continual dialogue about the meaning of the Christian faith and its implications for our lives. The chapters of this book began as sermons and have been amplified and reworked for wider circulation. My life has been richly blessed while serving this congregation.

By the Same Author

Living Stones

Starting Over Single

When Death Touches Your Life

Table of Contents

LET ME TELL YOU A STORY

Introduction

LET ME TELL YOU A STORY

I have always been fascinated by stories. In the good old days of my youth I remember snuggling up to the radio night after night absorbing many of the stories broadcast on that medium. One of the most intriguing parts of this experience was to use my imagination, to create in my mind the sounds, smells and colors that I believed were a part of that story. Radio always left a good deal to the imagination. We have lost much of that today with the advent of television. A story on the radio was more than a story, it was an entry into an entirely new world of fantasy and adventure.

I was also a prolific reader during those earlier years. My goal during a good portion of junior high was to check out a book from the library before school began in the morning and to have it read by the close of the day. That involved reading the book during some of the less exciting classes, an exercise not designed to curry favor from some teachers.

My favorite stories had to do with adventure, those that challenged the imagination to its greatest extent: Robinson Crusoe, Swiss Family Robinson, Gulliver's Travels, the Babe Ruth Story, The Robe, The Silver Chalice, and numerous books about the frontier in America by an author named Joseph Altsheller. Recently, I went looking for some of the books by Altsheller, and the library does not carry them anymore. I felt that something important had vanished.

Jesus understood our human appreciation for stories. He also lived in a culture where oral transmission of history and meaning was central to communication. Not much was written down, most was shared by word of mouth. Much of that sharing happened in story form.

Jesus also knew that theoretical teaching and abstract philosophizing often bores people to tears. But a story! A story relating to everyday life, unlike other kinds, can open up doors and windows. In addition, Jesus was a masterful story-teller. The stories in the New Testament are magnificent examples of teaching and interpretation. People always have a tendency to forget abstract doctrine, but a story can have an impact for a lifetime.

Jesus often answered questions by telling a story. The questions came fast and furious as He wandered throughout Palestine. Many of them went right to the heart of life's meaning. Jesus would respond to the questioner and to anyone else within earshot saying, "Let me tell you a story."

I base this book on the following presuppositions:

1. I believe that the parables are intensely theological. Many books and articles imply that the parables are basically for children, that they have little depth or meaning. Many theologians have basically skipped over the parables and quickly moved on to the weighty theological writings of Paul.

   I believe such reading of the parables is inadequate. Jesus is not throwing out some superficial nuggets to appeal to the simple minded: rather, he places into concrete form the very essence of the faith. All of the major themes that we confront in our search for meaning and purpose are here—death, resurrection, evangelism, social concern, forgiveness, justification, sanctification, the church—all of them. We can learn far more from a thorough look a the parables of Jesus than we might ever imagine.

2. The parables contain a revolutionary quality, a radical message which turns many of the accepted ideals and values of the day upside down. Time and again they are designed to shock, to provoke, to bring about an almost violent reaction from the crowd. They are guaranteed to offend almost everyone, as Jesus seeks to move the thinking and action of the people into an entirely new realm.

   In the parable of the Pharisee and the Publican, it is the latter who goes away justified. In the Good Samaritan, the solid religious folk walk by an injured man, crossing over to the other side, but the hated Samaritan stops to help. The message is clear, those who have been among the chosen, the "in" group, the elite, are not the ones who will be a part of the kingdom of God. Jesus is talking about a new order of things, where the first shall be last and the last first. The parables have a quality of feistiness about them, they cause people to challenge all of their prior assumptions.

3. Jesus uses the parables to talk about his own mission and ministry. Dr. Kenneth Bailey, a New Testament scholar who has spent most of his time in the Middle East and has most recently taught at a Presbyterian Seminary in Beruit, Lebanon, suggests that Jesus is often predicting his own death. A Samaritan who would have brought an injured Jew to an inn in first century society would have been in danger of losing his life. A son who demanded his inheritance would have been so hated by the community that his return would have been violently resisted, and possibly could have meant death.

   I have presented twelve of the parables in this book. There are many others that could have been included, which perhaps should be the subject of another book in the future. The amount of mining that can be done in the Gospels is endless, this is just a very humble beginning. My hope is that this preliminary work will be helpful to the reader, deepening one's faith and commitment and witness.

Special thanks needs to be given to my wife, Jackie, and children, Deanna and Noel. Without their constant encouragement and support I would not be able to undertake this effort of writing.

I also wish to express my gratitude to my parents, Conrad and Swanee Thompson, for their strong commitment to teaching their children "the story", and giving me access to so many written and oral stories.

I appreciate very much the leaders of our church during the

writing of this book: Lois Helvick, Mike Liton, Sharon Fetherhuff, and Paul Frederickson: as well as the other pastors on our staff: Richard Nelson, Ted Kalkwarf, and Doug Duin. My assistant, Mary Jeanne Benson has given invaluable help, as has Wayne Skaff, the director of our publishing company. This has been a team effort.

Chapter One

LET ME TELL YOU A STORY

BUILDING LIFE UPON THE ROCK

The Sermon on the Mount, found in Matthew 5-7, is full of picture language. Jesus uses some of the most illustrative and endearing word pictures in the entire Bible. Time and again Jesus probes the depth of truth and life by telling some very simple stories. This is his favorite teaching method, story-telling. Instead of composing volumes in the work of definition, he crafts beautiful, simple, graphic illustrations to portray clearly what he wants to communicate. As we see in these chapters of Matthew, Jesus tells more in a short story than most of us are able to say in a lifetime. Time after time, he focuses on a particular truth by using parables. All the way through the Gospels we hear Jesus saying to his listeners, "Let me tell you a story".

One of the most familiar of these pictures is presented in Matthew 7:24-27.

> "Therefore everyone who hears these words of mine and puts them into practice is like a wise man who built his house on the rock. The rain came down, the streams rose, and the winds blew and beat against that house; yet it did not fall, because it had its foundation on the rock. But everyone who hears these words of mine and does not put them into practice is like a foolish man who built his house on sand.

The rain came down, the streams rose, and the winds blew and beat against that house, and it fell with a great crash."

This parable reminds me of a story from my own life, from a long time ago.

There were just two of us, two little boys named Mark and Merv, accepting a challenge that is as old as time—creating a castle out of the acres of white sand encircling a glimmering northern Minnesota lake.

We took on this task with utmost seriousness, plotting and scheming like architects and engineers from the finest, most prestigious firm. We dreamed great dreams of building one of Europe's finest and most exquisite castles right there in the sand. A marvelous joy filled our preparations, and our imaginations soared to new heights as we surveyed the land and analyzed the water. Our creative juices ran wild! But before long, the time of planning became boring; it was now time to begin our work.

We joyfully launched into the unknown, not completely sure where we were going, but certain that nothing short of a masterpiece would emerge, rivaling even Michelangelo's work in the Sistine Chapel. We prepared the site without large earth moving machines, relying only on a couple of flimsy shovels and our bare hands. This was certainly our own creation.

We firmly packed the sand, mixing the driest of the sand with water to form a foundation that would not crumble. It seemed to us as firm as concrete, but of course it was anything but. We began our construction with the great wall, a huge structure more than a foot thick. It was designed to surround the entire castle compound, just like the one we had seen in the *National Geographic* on the coffee table at home.

I still remember the magnificence of that wall, reinforced with mud and stones in the most strategic places. After all, unless you have a wall such as this, how could you ever keep out the myriad of invaders who might come, such as turtles and puppydogs, sisters and baby brothers?

Inside the wall was the fanciest layout you could find. We arranged rooms this way and that way and created scores of windows overlooking the countryside. There were huge doors on the front of the castle and secret entrances and tunnels running throughout, giving it an aura of mystery.

In the midst of the entire complex we constructed the crown of our creation, the tower. Every castle worth its salt must have a tower, for how else could we detain prisoners or view the terrain for miles to watch for danger? Finally, we dug a formidable moat around the castle wall, wide enough so that marauding invaders could not scale the walls with ladders.

Our spanning of the centuries was most amazing, or amusing, depending upon your perspective. Next to the tenth century tower was a huge garage for our Cadillacs and Rolls Royces. In another part of the grounds was found our Olympic-sized swimming pool with a multi-level slide. Next to the great wall we had a landing strip for airplanes and a heliport for the helicopters. Historical inaccuracies did not bother us a bit, for we were only concerned with building our dream.

After several hours of hard work in the hot sun, we engineers tired of our colossal effort and decided that the cool water looked more inviting than the sand. Throwing down our shovels and placing our cars and trucks in the new castle garage, we wandered out into the lake. We agreed to return later to reinforce the walls, but that could wait. We knew we should also build a stronger foundation for the tower, but there would be time after a swim. The water was so inviting.

All of a sudden, the clouds rolled in, the wind began to blow, and the sky became very dark. Waves churned, dashing against the lakeshore. Two engineers immediately saw the potential for ruin and ran to save their creation.

Nothing could stop the wind and the water. The majestic castle wall began to crumble, the moat melted away. We piled our dump trucks and cars and shovels in the path of the water, but our efforts were too little and too late. The tower disintegrated as water rushed in from every side, methodically ripping our castle to pieces. Within moments there was nothing left—no building, no creation, just a memory.

Two builders stood with shovels in their hands and tears in their eyes, fighting back the sobs, overwhelmed that such a supreme creation could become a shambles. We promised to rebuild our dream castle another day, farther from the threatening lake, with a stronger foundation and a thicker wall. Our words were hollow, so empty. The castle had vanished.

Jesus is saying in his story that violent storms often appear in real life, not only in the playworld of children. Unless our own foundations are built on solid ground—on rock that will not crumble—our hopes and futures might wash away as quickly as the castle on the sand. Anyone who builds his or her life on the transitory and shifting sand will eventually slide into the stormy sea.

The image of the houses on the sand and on the rock has meaning for both adults and children. I believe we need to tell and retell this parable to our children, which means we must learn it by heart. One of the best ways to learn this parable is to sing the song:

> "The wise man built his house upon the rock/the wise man built his house upon the rock/the wise man built his house upon the rock, and the rains came tumbling down.
>
> The rains came down and the floods came up,/the rains came down and the floods came up,/the rains came down and the floods came up, but the house on the rock—stood firm.
>
> The foolish man built his house upon the sand,/the foolish man built his house upon the sand,/the foolish man built his house upon the sand, and the rains came tumbling down.

The rains came down and the floods came up,/the rains came down and the floods came up,/the rains came down and the floods came up, and the house on the sand—fell flat. (Clap your hands.)

So build your life on the Lord Jesus Christ,/build your life on he Lord Jesus Christ,/build your life on the Lord Jesus Christ, and the blessings will come down.

The blessings will come down as the prayers go up,/the blessings will come down as the prayers go up,/the blessings will come down as the prayers go up,/so build your life on Christ."

This story tells us that storms will certainly come to each of us; winds will blow fiercely against our lives. But if we build our lives on a solid foundation, if we center our focus and values on the rock, then we can never be washed away. "Built on the rock the Church Doth Stand", "Rock of Ages Cleft for Me". Life is found in the rock, for the rock is Christ.

In this story Jesus wants to make two distinct lifestyles, one positive and one negative, clear to us. It reminds me of a brother and sister I know well who loved to play the age-old game of hide and seek. They weren't interested so much in getting the best of each other as in meeting the challenge, mystery and intrigue of the sport. If other children in the neighborhood were available to play, well and good, but if not, then the two were content to play the game by themselves.

If adults were watching, they would be most interested to see how each child seemed to play according to a different set of rules and expectations. The little girl believed that the primary goal was to avoid being found. She would search for that perfect place to hide, not exposing her hiding place to anyone. Even if everyone else quit the game and went elsewhere, she would stay right there in her hiding place, never moving a muscle, never making a sound. She would almost quit breathing so as not to tip off the searchers. She wanted, above all, to be lost. Sometimes adults had to intervene and even plead, "The game is over. Please come out!"

Her brother was just the opposite. He wanted above all to be found. To him it was a waste of valuable time to sit in silence waiting to be discovered. That ranked right up there with taking a bath or eating spinach. He would do almost anything to be detected quickly. If he had to wait too long he would make little noises, peek from behind the chair or the closet door, clear his throat or begin to cough. Sometimes he even ran from one hiding place to another, a sure way to be discovered in hide and seek. He was never very difficult to find. His goal was to be found, and he was very, very good at that.

I wonder if these two styles are not similar to what Jesus has in mind when he talks about the rock and the sand, the wise and the foolish. Clearly it seems that some people work very diligently at being lost. They build their lives on sand, even on quicksand. Everyone around them can see that they are headed in the wrong direction, that disaster looms nearby. It is like building on the precarious sand, waiting for the first serious storm.

There are others, however, who spend their lives trying to be found. They build their lives on rock that cannot be moved even by hurricanes or tornados. The storms come to them just as frequently as to the people living on the sand, there is never any quarantee of avoiding the high waters and the gale-force winds. Yet they are able to sing the great hymn of the church, "On Christ the solid rock I stand; all other ground is sinking sand."

A wealthy developer made his fortune by designing and constructing single-family homes in a fast-growing suburban community. He built thousands of homes over a 20 year period — high quality, reasonably priced homes. One of his best employees was a construction superintendent who had been intimately involved in the building of the majority of these homes. This employee was an especially gifted and experienced master craftsman, his credentials were of the highest order.

As the developer grew older, he began to spend more and more time in Florida during the winter months. One year during the late fall he decided to go south for the longest stay yet, so he called in his trusted employee to give him instructions. He said to him,

> "You have worked for me for a long time, and your service and loyalty have been excellent all these years. I know you to be faithful and trustworthy. While I am gone this winter, I want you to build a special home for me. I want it to be the finest you have ever constructed. Use the best materials, hire the best crew. Be very careful, quality is much more important than cost. You are on your own, and I expect the finest home you have ever built when I return."

The superintendent went to work immediately, but as he became involved with the project, it suddenly came to him that he could make a great deal of extra money by using inferior construction materials. Of course he would use them where no one could see them; there should be no problem with this. He would get by with his deception scot-free.

He ordered marginal lumber. Where he should have used two by sixes, he used rather scrawny two by fours. Where he should have used good, solid three-quarter inch plywood, he used the cheaper half-inch. Where he should have used top-grade insulation, he used some inferior quality which simply could not do the job. And where he should have used the best piping on the market, he installed poor materials there as well. Though the house looked sensational on the outside, the infrastructure was inferior.

When the developer returned from his vacation, he drove out right away to look at this dream house. He expected something extraordinary, and he was not disappointed. As far as he could tell, the design was both original and superb, the workmanship was excellent, the finishing exquisite. He praised the employee for the excellence of the work, as well as for his faithfulness and loyalty throughout the years.

Then with tears in his eyes, the developer said to his trusted worker, "In gratefulness for your many years of service, I want to give you the keys to this new home. It is yours! You, of all people, deserve it."

In a sense, this is what happens to each of us. We are given instructions to build our lives with care and respect, and to build them on a lasting foundation. But ocassionally we are tempted to turn to the cheap and inferior, to throw away our time and energy and values and physical well-being on that which is empty and transitory. We major in minors. We waste our God-given talents and abilities. Unfortunately, when we build our lives on inferior foundations and sinking sand, we often have to live with these decisions for the rest of our lives.

I know a high school student who played her way through school. She rarely took a course that challenged her intellect. She only valued the pleasures of the moment. "Let the future take care of itself," she quipped ever so glibly. She had no roots, no foundation, no stability at all. Friends who were building strong foundations soon drifted away from her, so she could only play with a different crowd.

One day shortly after high school was over, she woke to find wind and rain lashing against her life, and there was nothing around her but sand—miles and miles of sand, sinking and washing away all around her. With a crash, her life caved in. It has taken many years for her to get her head above water again and overcome that tragedy. There is the possibility that she might not make it. God-willing there is now hope.

Another high school student whom I know built his life on drugs. His foundation almost made sand look solid. When he was not stoned, life was boring and meaningless to him. Then again, when he was high, he fooled himself into believing that life was good and he was unbeatable.

But the storms did come. And how they came! They battered him at every turn. He wasn't strong enough to withstand them and landed in the hospital. His dreams, body, mind and spirit broke apart. His house built on the sand fell flat.

I know a young couple who thought they were madly in love at the ripe old age of sixteen. For each of them, the sun rose and fell on just one other person. Schoolwork, friendships, church and family were shoved aside, because all that mattered was the time these young suitors spent with each other. They walked through high school in a romantic swoon, in a fog that never lifted. They believed that their love was the strongest foundation for the future that they could have.

A storm soon came, the winds gained hurricane force, and they were unprotected. They had no friends, no family, no education, no faith, no vacation, just some vague feelings of love and affection for each other. When they fell, they fell very hard, and life came crashing down on them.

Jesus says in the story, build your lives on the rock, on that which is lasting, on a foundation which will not crumble, which will not fall apart when the storms come. We all know the storms will come to us, they always do. We need to build our lives on the rock, and that rock is Jesus Christ. "Built on the rock the church does stand." Built on the rock, we too can stand. If Christ is at the center of our lives, we will never be washed away by the storms.

I know another teenager whose goal has been to build and maintain his solid foundation on the rock. He worked hard in school, taking classes which stretched him and forced him to grow, even classes which he did not like or which did not come easy for him. He spent quality time with his family, he sang in his church choir, he spent a summer working with disadvantaged children. All through his formative years his faith in Jesus Christ became more real.

Everyone who looked at him would say that he was building a strong foundation for the future. His life was filled with opportunities and open doors, not because life was always easy, but because he would not quit until the doors opened. Why did it happen? Because he chose to build on the rock instead of on the sand. He built carefully and confidently, using the best materials instead of relying on cheap imitations.

The modern day storyteller and child philosopher, Dr. Seuss, says it as well as anyone:

> "If you'd never been born, then what would you be? You might be a fish or a toad in a tree, you might be a doorknob or three baked potatoes, worse than all that, you might be a wasn't. A wasn't has no fun at all! No, he doesn't! A wasn't just isn't! He isn't present. But you—you are you!
>
> Now isn't that present. Today you are you and it's truer than true. That there's no one alive who is you'er than you! Shout loud! 'I am lucky to be what I am!' Thank goodness I'm not just a clam or a ham! Or a dusty old jar of gooseberry jam. I am what I am and it's a great thing to be, if I say so myself, happy birthday to me!"

One day the young man who had built his life on the rock was out walking in the woods after a snowstorm. He heard noises behind him. Looking back, he saw a young boy following him. He called to him, "What are you doing out here?" The child replied, "Please walk carefully, I am following in your footsteps."

We must also walk carefully because people are following in our footsteps.

What kind of a life are we building? Are we using the best materials, the solid, dependable and lasting kind? Are we "growing deep and strong," to paraphrase a book title by Karen Kaiser Clark? Or are we constructing our lives out of the scraps, the leftovers that will blow away in the storm?

Jesus said, "The wise person builds on the rock and the foolish person builds on the sand." Which kind of builder are you?

THE EXTRAVAGANT GRACE OF GOD AND THE GRACELESSNESS OF THE CROWD

Most embarrassing moments are "in". Television finds a kind of voyeristic fascination with parading the forgettable moments of people's lives. In real life, people are both fascinated and repelled by episodes involving people who would have given anything for a hole in which to hide. Red-faced, stammering, horrifying moments are all too real to most of us, sometimes providing both humor and regret, albeit not always in equal portions. Embarrasment is another one of those givens in life, sometimes useful, sometimes upsetting, sometimes humanizing.

The event that is recorded in the 7th chapter of Luke, verses 36-39 is one such embarassing moment. The particular facial expressions of the participants, the body language, the righteous indignation would have added drama for observers. Without any videotaping crew present, however, we must listen to the words of the passage, imagining the absolute horror and shock that must been present.

"Now one of the Pharisees invited Jesus to have dinner with him, so he went to the Pharisee's house, and reclined at the table. When a woman who had lived a sinful life in that town learned that Jesus was eating at the Pharisee's house, she brought an alabaster jar of perfume, and as she stood before him at his feet weeping, she began to wet his feet with her tears. Then she wiped them with her hair, kissed them and poured perfume on them.

When the Pharisee who had invited him saw this, he said to himself, "If this man were a prophet, he would know what is touching him and what kind of a woman she is . . . that she is a sinner."

Another translation, The living Bible, calls her a prostitute. In any event, by any standard, rampant embarrassment is at work in this scene.

Let's put ourselves into this first century scene for a moment. We have been invited by a prominent man named Simon to a dinner party. Simon holds particular respect and honor from among the guests and the community as a whole because of special virtue and impeccable morals. He is a Pharisee. Why Jesus would appear as a special guest in this household is beyond my imagination. The gulf between social classes is wide enough to be impassable. In addition, Jesus often verbally battles with the Pharisees. Perhaps Simon shared some affinity though, both in action and in ultimate concern, with another Pharisee named Nicodemus, who had sought Jesus in the middle of the night. Perhaps Simon too wanted to know something about eternal life. Maybe he was not all that different from you and me.

Let's peek around at the setting. Simon had prepared no small, insignificant dining hall for this encounter. Apparently, a substantial number of guests are present. Nothing is spared for such an occasion. The food, the drink, the conversation, and the people are carefully chosen. Opportunities for memorable events do not appear all that frequently, and life-changing scenarios appear olny rarely. However, this celebration provided the open door for a "kairos" event, an "aha" moment with long-term impact.

As the servants scurry around with the final preparations, as the smells permeate the banquet hall at the highpoint of the meal, a wild commotion interrupts the serenity of that evening. Smashing into the tranquility and good conversation comes a pathetic looking woman, wild-eyed, weeping, thrashing about. Suddenly she is throwing herself at the feet of Jesus, babbling on endlessly. Nothing is clear during this moment of excruciating tension. Why has this woman come to this feast? What does she want Jesus to do for her? Most importantly, how can she be ushered out before eveything is ruined?

Just imagine the embarrassment, the shock, the anger! A woman of the street rushing into a dinner party filled with good and moral and respectable people. Speechlessness must have been deafening. Frustration was pervasive. Then suddenly the crowd became nasty.

"Get her out of here!" The shouts crescendoed through the room. "Get her out of here. How did such trash get in here, anyway, throw her out! We have never been so mortified and insulted in our whole lives, chase her away!" The vigilantes among them were already beginning to rise in their chairs. The next act would have been to carry this woman kicking and screaming out of that place. If television cameras had been present, it would have been better than most prime time material

The woman, however, had one last action to perform before the violent wheels of Middle Eastern first century justice took over. Firmly grabbing an alabaster jar of ointment from her clothing, she proceeded to pour it all over the feet of Jesus. Valuable perfume, nothing cheap about it, the kind that was a symbol of wealth and privilege, poured over the feet of this itinerant teacher and prophet. Amidst shouts from all over the room, a woman sobbed uncontrollably as she wiped the feet of Jesus with her hair. Embarrassment reeked throughout the crowd.

Simon the Pharisee must have been the most appalled. After all, this had occurred on his watch, He was scandalized. This happened in his house. How would he ever recover from this trauma and public humiliation? Unfortunately he reached back into his grab bag of responses and chose one that is intimately familiar to each of us. He did what any good, red-blooded person would do, even in our own age, or especially in our own time. He looked around for a scapegoat. There has to be someone at fault. It served no real purpose to blame this helpless, distraught woman: he needed a much better target. Amazingly, he had the perfect foil, and so do we. His name is Jesus.

Without question, this sorry affair was the fault of Jesus. If Jesus only would have known the kind of woman this was who came bursting into the house, he would not have permitted such a scene. Simon declares that this is Jesus' fault. There was no problem in society that might have contributed to this situation, there was no blame whatsoever in any other guest in the house, obviously and inevitably, Jesus'.

Surprisingly, or perhaps not so surprisingly, not much has changed from the first to the 20th century. The enterprise of scapegoating is still a favorite sport among people in our time. We have developed alarming expertise in the art of blaming someone else for anything in the world that has gone wrong. With much of our fragile world, crumbling or exploding at any one time, scapegoating can cetainly become a full-time obsession. How comforting to focus blame on someone else, rather than to take any kind of personal responsibility.

Examples abound. When something negative happens in a person's life, no matter how small it might be, a common temptation is to blame the government. It is the president's fault; it is the fault of Congress. No doubt our leadership can rightly accept blame for a whole host of problems and situations in our nation and world, but the kind of scapegoating that goes on in this arena is beyond belief. Perhaps instead of national leaders, it is God's fault, or someone "out there" Ready targets for blame are always available.

Scapegoating has become so pervasive that we even tend to blame victims for what happens to them. When a wife is battered about by an abusive male, often she is blamed for somehow provoking the attack. The same judgment frequently has been made in terms of rape. The actions of the woman are somehow responsible for the violent act. Poor people are often made the scapegoat for their condition by society, obviously they should be blamed for abject poverty.

Humanity is so often predictable, and one of the most common traits is our propensity to blame others for our problems. Somebody else is at fault, and someone had better pay. Lawsuit heaven describes our nation at present because we want to find people to blame. We have more lawyers per square inch than any other locale on the face of the earth.

I heard one humorist with tongue-in-cheek suggest that he had found the solution to our preoccupation with suing our neighbor. For every Japanese car that is sold in this country—Honda, Toyota, Nissan, etc.—we will send Japan one lawyer. That is funny to everyone but lawyers, of course, but it highlights something of the reality of our use of scapegoating.

I heard about a man recently who was burglarizing a business somewhere in the southwestern part of the United States. While climbing around on the roof of a company, trying to find a way in illegally, he fell through one of the skylights and was seriously injured. This would-be burglar then sued the company that he was trying to rob, and stranger than that, the jury awarded him substantial compensation for his injuries. The fault, obviously, was with the business, not with the man. Give me a scapegoat!

Jesus knew exactly what was transpiring in the hearts and minds of the people in the room. When the woman crashed the party, Jesus understood completely the feelings and frustrations that were involved. This was certainly a teachable moment, although it could be argued that the lessons of that day would be more easily assimilated by this crowd at a later date, rather than in the heat of the moment. But Jesus thought it was the right time to teach, so he said to them, "Let me tell you a story."

The words are found in Luke 7:41-50.

> "Jesus begins, 'Two men owed money to a certain moneylender. One owed him five hundred denarii, and the other fifty. Neither of them had the money to pay him back, so he cancelled the debts of both. Now which of them will love him more?'
>
> Simon replied, 'I suppose the one who had the bigger debt cancelled.' 'You have judged correctly,' Jesus said. Then he turned toward the woman and said to Simon, 'Do you see this woman? I came into your house. You did not give me any water for my feet, but she wet my feet with her tears and wiped them with her hair.
>
> You did not give me a kiss but she has not stopped kissing my feet. You did not put oil on my head, but she has poured perfume on my feet. Therefore, I tell you, her many sins have been forgiven, for she loved much. But he who has been forgiven little loves little.'
>
> Then Jesus said to her, 'Your sins are forgiven.' The other guests began to say among themselves, 'Who is this who even forgives sins?' Jesus said to the woman, 'Your faith has saved you; go in peace.' "

This story abounds with meaning and truth and application to our own lives. In essence, Jesus is affirming that forgiveness is among the most precious gifts in the world; indeed in his own life he will demonstrate its value by giving his very life. A basic principle also is implied, that very often those who are most in the need of forgiveness are most welcome and appreciative of the gift.

In other words, often those who have sunk deepest into the mire are the most enthusiastic and exuberant when delivered from the abyss. The prodigal son seems much more grateful than the elder brother.

Another prime example must be the woman who washes Jesus' feet with her hair and her tears. She was so desperate, so despised and rejected, that she was willing to risk the displeasure and even violence of the crowd in order to plead for forgiveness and love. What a testimony to the power of divine love, to the visible evidence of God's affirming acceptance of all who come to him! Even a person with the moral bankruptcy of this person can experience the unequivocable and unlimited forgiveness of God in Jesus Christ!

Many themes are woven into the fabric of this story. Let's consider three.

The Extravagance of God

The story of Jesus and his personal example of compassion and love for this troubled woman demonstrates in a dramatic way the overwhelming grace of God. A strong case could be made that this is the overriding theme of the Gospels and of the Christian faith—a passionate, immeasurable, eternal outpouring of God's grace.

Extravagance is the catchword permeating this scene. Just as the woman pours out a container of expensive perfume over Jesus' feet, in a far greater sense God pours out the costly perfume of new life and forgiveness. Extravagance is a recurring theme. In another instance the water is changed into wine, not just a gallon or two, but more than 180 gallons of wine. Amazing grace.

In the feeding of the five thousand, when twelve baskets of food are left over, we see another picture of God's life-giving love. Still another dramatic image is found in that magnificent event of the loving father welcoming home the tragic figure of his son, a son who had tried to gain the whole world, but had lost everything.

Not everything, however. He had not lost the boundless seeking love of the father, the love of almighty God.

Scripture, time and again, provides something like a chorus, a never-ending rendition of "Amazing Grace", when God gives beyond measure, pressed down, shaken together, running over. Martin Luther declares that all of this giving is without any merit or worthiness on our part, but is purely a gift from a gracious God. Standing above all other gifts, of course, is the cross, the surpreme gift of God, Jesus Christ. For God so loved the world that he gave...How much? That he gave his only begotten Son. What a resounding chorus of such extravagant love!

This is our calling, to love and give extravagantly. In Matthew 5, Jesus tells all who follow to be extravagant when responding to this divine love. He tells us to go one mile and then to go the second mile and the third and the fourth. Forgive not only seven times, but seventy times seven. Pray often, but not only that, pray without ceasing. Certainly give your coat, but see how much more you can give, give your cloak as well. Extravagant loving giving is our calling. It was also the calling of the destitute widow who gave everything that she had (Luke 21:1-4).

Contrast this calling to the way we so often live. If there is any description which characterizes most of us in terms of giving it is this, "Be careful! Take every precaution, don't reach out to another until you are absolutely sure. Use the measuring stick, don't take any risks. Watch out, be careful, we don't want anyone going overboard on this giving stuff, we don't want to be embarrassed by someone who gives unconditionally. Be careful, take it easy, hold tight to what you have, be careful before you leap, be very, very cautious!"

I wonder if this also does not become our 'modus operandi' in terms of our relationships with others. Be careful, we remind ourselves, be very careful, don't get too close, don't get involved in the live of others. Be cautious, don't place your feet too firmly in the hurts and needs of others.

I talked with a man recently who told me that two neighbors had moved away in recent months. All three families had been close for a dozen years or more. He was most upset by this turn of events; in a sense he was grieving over this loss. Now he said to me, "I don't think I will invest myself again in the lives of others as I did with these friends. It is just not worth it. People will only move away again."

The temptation to live our lives with a series of contingencies is never far away. We can always bail out if things get too uncomfortable or if someone moves too close to us. Be careful, don't pour yourself too permanently into anything—marriage, family, work, the church! Be careful, give a little, get a lot! Stay cool, stay close to the fringe, keep those boundaries intact. Be so very careful.

Detachment has not provided for our deepest needs, it has rather brought us estrangement and isolation. Instead of protecting us from hurt and pain, it has kept us from experiencing much of the joy and wonder of life. There is no ultimate risk in being extravagant, for we always gain back far more than we invest in others. Jesus' life is the example, disciples become risk takers. Let the extravagance of God shine through each of us. What a different world it would be?

A top ten favorite of our children when they were in kindergarten was the song that went something like this:

Love isn't love until you give it away,
  give it away, give it away
Love isn't love until you give it away,
  and you'll end up having more.
Love is like a shiny penny.
  Hold it tight and you won't have any,
Lend it, spend it, and you'll have so many
  they'll roll all over the floor, oh!
Love isn't love until you give it away,

and you'll end up having more.

In the final analysis, our lives should be filled with examples of a selfless, giving for the sake of others, extravagance, not so much because of what we do, but because of what is done for us. God's gifts to us provide the pattern for this overflowing grace. Just the other day we received a beautiful note from our daughter Deanna as she left on a trip. In a special way, the note said, "I love you."

Another blessing filled moment came as we gathered with some special fiends for a surprise birthday party—what serendipity! There is that walk at sunset, the view of the mountains, the special dinner with just my wife, Jackie, and myself, the kindness and thoughtfulness of our son Noel in a gift he gave to us. The circles grow wider, as notes of encouragement pour in from friends in our congregation at a time of illness. Extravagance never ends!

What we need in this troubled world of ours is a community of people who are willing to respond to the extravagant grace of God with an outpouring of love and giving. Risking for others needs to replace being so all-blooming careful. It sometimes means getting out of the boat and launching out into the deep.

Perhaps our response should center in tithing, in giving of all that we have, even more than the ten percent. Maybe it involves traveling across the seas or across the street to do some missionary work, sharing the love of Jesus. Or it could mean sitting with another person for many hours, sharing the pain and sorrow that is a part of life.

Many of us live in such affluence today, even though we have trouble making ends meet. Extravagance for its own sake is self-defeating, but extravagance on behalf of others, and in the name of the kingdom of God is revolutionary. The world reaches out for an extravagant response to an extravagant God.

The Reality of Evil

This theme comes through loud and clear. Sometimes we are so easily caught up in the joy of forgiveness that we forget the tragedy of the evil in the story. There are many kinds of evil represented in the parable. Not the least is the sin of the woman and those who used and abused her.

I'm reminded of a book from a few years back by Dr. Karl Menninger, in which he asks the pointed question, *What Ever Became of Sin?* His analysis in the book was that we have attempted to basically explain sin away, to psychologize it, to call it something else. And soon we have concluded that there is no sin left. Just by changing language, we sometimes believe we have eliminated sin.

Jesus would sharply remind us that none of us dare underestimate the power of evil. All around us in our world we can see some of the tragedy that is caused by the reality of sin, how many people live in perpetual misery and inhuman conditions. Television parades in front of us examples of this evil; hunger, war, apartheid, terrorism, poverty, discrimination, persecution. Our list of evidences of evil would be far too long for just one book. Evil is pervasive, everywhere present, all around us. We sometimes believe that if we become more civilized, evil will disappear. The civilized Nazis of World War II should forever dissuade us of this myth.

The Bible deals with the reality of evil from the very first book of the Bible, in fact in the first chapters of Genesis. Again there is a story, and this story is not so much about the origin of evil as it is about the way evil dominates and destroys the lives of human beings. There is no more moving account of the reality of evil than in the first three chapters of the Bible.

Genesis, chapters one and two, begins with some beautiful words about a garden and paradise and a magnificent creation. "God saw that it was good." But in the third chapter we find we find the evil dominating all existence, scandulous, destructive, and pervasive. The words from Genesis 3:8-13 are most graphic.

> "Then the man and his wife heard the sound of the Lord God as he was walking in the garden in the cool of the day, and they hid from the Lord God among the trees of the garden. But the Lord God called to the man, 'Where are you?'
>
> He answered, 'I heard you in the garden, and I was afraid because I was naked; so I hid.' And he said, 'Who told you that you were naked? Have you eaten from the tree that I commanded you not to eat from?'
>
> The man said, 'The woman you put here with me—she gave me some fruit from the tree, and I ate it.' Then the Lord God said to the woman, 'What is this you have done?' The woman said, 'The serpent deceived me, and I ate.'"

How can evil be associated with Adam and Eve? They were most likely two very nice people, the kind of folks who would fit very comfortably into a lifestyle such as ours. No doubt they would be exemplary neighbors, certainly maintaining an impressive garden. Faith in God would be especially central to their family life. They are basically hard-working, responsible people. Like most of us, they had all they needed, all the basics. Also like us, they wanted more. Having it all, they wanted more.

The story of Adam and Eve suggests from the very beginning of time that the origin of evil comes from a very basic premise, common to most of humankind. When people believe that they do not have enough, that there is something more they simply must have, then all sorts of evil begins to creep into the center of life. Convinced that we do not have enough, greed and envy and lust overcome us and equip us for rationalizing away some of the worst kinds of evil.

Adam and Eve highlight a profound feeling that is present in so many of us. Deep in the center of our being we sense that we don't have everything we should have. Something crucial to our happiness and well-being is missing. We can't always identify what it is, yet we want to go for it. Instead of dwelling on our blessings, on all that we have, we concentrate on what we do not have. The Bible instructs us to not covet or steal or kill or commit adultery. The evil comes so often when we believe we do not have enough that we will do almost anything to satisfy that urge.

Not surprisingly, Adam and Eve were wide open to the alluring and tempting voice of evil, Adam and Eve, you can have it all, whenever you want it, all the time. God has set some limits for you, some limits in your garden, but just this once, go for it! As long as you don't hurt anyone else, why not? After all, God's limits are dated, they may have been appropriate in the past, but not for now. Adam and Eve, you are getting older, you are reaching a mid-life crisis, so just once, eat from the tree, do something for yourself, take care of Number One. So we find that Adam and Eve are as ripe as the fruit of the tree, ripe for temptation and betrayal and evil. They feel deep inside that what they have and are is not enough.

A day of reckoning comes quickly, Adam and Eve are suddenly jolted into a shocking awareness of their sin and evil. Notice what action they take—they hide. Filled with a sense of horror because of their disobedience, they hide. When God asked them why they were hiding, they alibied by pointing to their nakedness. Clearly they were naked, in much more than a physical sense, standing there with all of the greed and envy and evil uncovered. I am sure they felt very cold.

Our experience is not all that different. We too have a tendency to hide when we are hounded by guilt. We hide behind many different things—work, play, chemicals, maybe even the church. God wants to meet us face to face, but we too often hide. When evil is discovered in us, when embarrassment is present, our most common human response is to hide. How many of us are hiding even today?

Hiding is never effective. Adam and Eve must own up to their sin. Adam had the classic answer. It went something like, "Lord, it really was not my fault. Don't look at me, I am not to blame. It was the woman who caused all of this mess! Look at Eve, in fact when I think of it you were the one who gave her to me! Perhaps it is even your fault. That's it, the presence of evil is your fault, Lord. Don't blame me!"

Sounds alarmingly familiar, like the Pharisee named Simon at the dinner, scapegoating, blaming someone else. Once again the oldest response in the world is whipped into action, pointing out the slivers in the eyes of others, rather than owning up to the logs in our own eyes. As American as apple pie, the evil in this world is not our fault, we have no responsibility for sin, it is caused by others. We might even declare with Adam, "Lord you created this mess; maybe it is your fault." Adam blames his wife and he blames God, how contemporary!

We can't forget about Eve. No dominant-subordinate stuff going on in her; she is liberated. She speaks right up, "Now wait a minute, God, the problem is not with me, I am blameless in all of this. The cause is that serpent who tempted me. Lord, the devil made me do this. I mean, I could not help myself, I am without blame."

Evil always has tragic consequences. God declares to Adam and Eve that in choosing evil over good, they have set a painful course for themselves and for their descendants. Evil will exact a tremendous cost for us all. Nowhere is this more evident than in the life of their two sons, when Cain kills Abel. Evil becomes universal.

William Willimon in his book *Sighing For Eden,* says that evil is organic, it feeds on itself. Evidence abounds all around us, illustrating that one sin leads to two, two leads to four and it multiplies rapidly.

For example, most of those in our day who are being prosecuted for child abuse were abused as children. The sins of the parents being passed on to future generations. Perhaps the prostitute in the dramatic events of Luke 7 had also been abused as a child. Perhaps she was a victim of her childhood.

Simon and the other Pharisees' responses are predictable. They want her out. Becoming judge and jury, she is convicted and the key already thrown away in the minds of the crowd. Forgiveness—never! Compassion—forget it! A willingness to listen and understand—not on your life! To become one with the Pharisees today tempts each of us, to hold back our heads a bit, to look down our noses at some persons or groups—to write them off, to condemn.

People are so often labeled, treated like lepers, isolated from the mainstream of life. I remember one summer when our son's soccer team played a team from England. The boys on this visiting team had all managed to visit the same overly-zealous barber, who had left them only enough hair on their heads to be seen at very close range.

As could be expected, the boys on our team were thoroughly amused by the hair styles of their opponents, making fun of them, calling them skinheads and all of that. It was terribly funny to our team, that is, until the other team came out and dominated us to the tune of six to zero.

Jesus had no interest in labels, in stereotypes, in scapegoating, only in persons. His purpose was not to generate a litany of sins from the past, but only to show the extravagant love of God to each person. Thus the words, "Do not stop them, for such is the kingdom of God." Mark 10:14 "Come unto me all who are weary and burdened, and I will give you rest." Matthew 11:28

Get rid of the labels, Jesus is saying. This woman may have lived a horrible life, but I forgive her, I will give her the power and will to start over again. The answer to the evil of the world is not judgment and hatred, but rather love. Perfect love casts out fear. On the cross, Jesus defeated the power of evil. Now we embrace that gift of love. What extravagant grace, even for a person like this woman!

Forgiveness

This story centers on the immeasurable power of forgiveness. The woman who poured her perfume over Jesus' feet and washed them with her hair undoubtedly believed inside that she was worth absolutely nothing, that she was the scum of the earth. Some people today try and call prostitution a "victimless crime." What a sham! The suicide rate among prostitutes is obscene: the very personhood of these victims is stripped away!

Yet Jesus offers forgiveness. In spite of her past, Jesus is willing to forgive. What a transformation! Forgiveness is the most revolutionary and life-changing word and action in this world. The opportunity to start all over again is a miracle of rebirth. Jesus offers this gift to each of us. "Your sins are forgiven, pick up your bed and walk," (John 5:8). Forgiveness is the greatest force in the world, more powerful than military might, bombs or missiles.

The story originated on a subway wall in the heart of New York City. A huge advertising poster decorated that wall, depicting a very dignified older man in a suit and vest and top hat, recommending a certain brand of cigarette. However, someone had come along with a magic marker, probably a small boy, and had written some words in bold letters.

Reaching deep inside of himself to find the nastiest thing he could use to deface the poster, the boy finally wrote next to the dignified man, "I like girls, I like girls." Spelling was not one of this youngster's most developed skills, so he wrote the words, "I like grils. I like grils." The poster remained like this for some time, with the distinguished man spouting the words, "I like grils."

Later, another person had come along and observed the writing on the poster. Deciding that some corrective action needed to be taken, to set the record straight, this person added the words just underneath the scrawling by the first defacer, "It's girls, stupid, not grils." In bold letters of the magic marker, "It's girls, stupid, not grils."

The poster was becoming rather cluttered by this time, but still a third person came along who believed that all had not been said to the viewing public. Therefore, underneath where the other word had been written, this budding philospher wrote, "But what about us grils?" But what about us grils? In one form or another, a similar question confronts so many of us today. What about all of us who are grils? What about all those who seem to be crowded out of life, those whom nobody seems to notice, or to care about? What about all of those who have been pushed aside, who are out of the mainstream, who believe they have little or no self worth? What about all the grils of a troubled world?

I talked to a nineteen-year-old young man recently who basically said to me, "I am a gril. I have no true friends, I can't get a decent job. I have nothing to live for. I am a gril."

A woman in a nursing home said to me, "I just sit here all of the time. Hardly anyone comes to see me. I have no worth. I would be better off dead. I am a gril."

Many high school students have said the same words in one way or another, "I am a gril. I want to be a superstar in something, I want others to notice me and respect me, but I am so plain and average, I never excel in anything. I am a gril."

A man who lost his job after seventeen years of faithful service said to me, "I am a gril. I don't even want to leave my house during the day, I don't want to see anybody. I am worth nothing. I am a gril."

A woman whose husband walked out after twenty-five years of marriage said,"I am a gril. I am all alone now, my children have moved away, my husband has left. Life has lost all meaning for me. I am a gril."

Everywhere we look we find grils. Sometimes we even catch a glimpse of a gril when we look in the mirror. For those who know what it means to be a gril, we understand how much it hurts. It hurts right down in the middle of our stomach, right in the center of our being. It hurts to be a gril. It hurts enough to make you cry. To be a gril is to feel out of it, to wonder if anybody truly cares, to see the rest of the world going by without you, to wonder why you are here.

George Gobel once quipped about grils, "Do you ever feel like the whole world is a freeway, and you are an off ramp? Do you ever feel like the whole world is a black tuxedo and you are a pair of brown shoes?" Do you ever feel like a gril?

The tragic woman in Luke 7 is a gril. She has been pushed out, rejected, abused, and excommunicated from society. But Jesus' response to her, and to every gril is one of unconditional acceptance and love. Forgiveness is the greatest power in the world. It is the power to start over again, to find that we are truly loved, to find value and dignity in life.

We have explored three themes in this parable, the extravagance of grace, the pervasiveness of evil, and the miracle of forgiveness. Each of these words is crucial to our lives under the Lordship of Jesus Christ.

WHAT TO DO WITH ALL OF THOSE TALENTS

God has given to each of us all of the gifts that we could possibly ever need, as difficult to believe as that may be for some. These are priceless gifts, far beyond what we could ever imagine or deserve. You and I are so gifted, so amazingly talented, that it defies our imagination. The creativity, the wisdom, the intuition, the common sense that we possess is simply unbelievable.

The body of Christ, the Church, also overflows with gifts and talents. Every congregation, almost without exception, has all of the resources it needs to carry out the mission of Christ in this world. We have been literally filled to the brim with these manifold talents, even to the point of overflowing.

Sometimes it becomes a favorite indoor sport to whine about our gifts and talents. "Lord," we say, "if only you would have given me more resources, if only you would have filled me with the kind of talents that I see present in others around me, then life would have been so rich and full. If only, if only, if only."

Self-pity and helplessness often take up residence inside each of us and within our Christian community. Actions based on such feelings even become self-fulfilling at times, for example, the more helpless we feel, the more helpless we become. Jesus declares unequivocably, that each of us has been given many diverse talents and gifts, more than we can imagine, more than we believe we have, more than we deserve, more than we can use in a lifetime! We are not empty vessels when we are born, nor do we remain empty. We are filled with possibilities and open doors.

Jesus also makes it abundantly clear that these gifts are meant to be used. We often get a lot of mileage from talking about "potential"; we like to examine and to contemplate our potential. Children are often viewed in this light as coaches will evaluate athletes on their potential.

Yet potential is not the key to unlocking our talents. All sorts of people are walking around with amazing potential, but they never use it. Jesus says that gifts are meant to be used, developed, stretched, and shared with the world. Many Christians over the centuries have taken their gifts and talents and fled to the countryside, spending lifetimes in monasteries or hideaways. This action is foreign to Jesus' teaching about gifts. They are meant to be used, not hidden in the ground or stored in some remote fallout shelter.

One day Jesus was instructing the disciples on the use and investment of their talents when he said to them, "Let me tell you a story." Matthew 25:14-27:

> "Again, it will be like a man going on a journey, who called his servants and entrusted his property to them. To one he gave five talents of money, to another two talents, and to another one talent, each according to his own ability. Then he went on his journey.
>
> The man who had received the five talents went at once and put his money to work and gained five more. So also, the one with the two talents gained two more. But the man who had received the one talent went off, dug a hole in the ground and hid his master's money.
>
> After a long time the master of those servants returned and settled accounts with them. The man who had received

the five talents brought the other five. 'Master,' he said, 'you entrusted me with five talents. See, I have gained five more.' His master replied, 'Well, done, good and faithful servant! You have been faithful with a few things; I will put you in charge of many things. Come and share your master's happiness!'

The man with the two talents also came. 'Master,' he said, 'you entrusted me with two talents: see, I have gained two more.' His master replied, 'Well done, good and faithful servant! You have been faithful with a few things: I will put you in charge of many things. Come and share your master's happiness!'

Then the man who had received the one talent came. 'Master,' he said, 'I knew that you are a hard man, harvesting where you have not sown and gathering where you have not scattered seed. So I was afraid and went out and hid your talent in the ground. See, here is what belongs to you.'

His master replied, 'You wicked, lazy servant! So you know that I harvest where I have not sown and gather where I have not scattered seed? Well then, you should have put my money on deposit with the bankers, so that when I returned I would have received it back with interest.'"

A paraphrase of this story may shed new light.

There was a master who gave three of his servants some very large and magnificent gifts. Each of the servants received the generous gifts, not just the first and the second of the servants. To the first man he gave five talents, to the second he gave two, and to the third he gave one. Each of these talents was far beyond what any of the servants had any right to expect, far beyond what they deserved, it was theirs only because of the grace and generosity and compassion of the giver.

These gifts were not meant to be thrown away, to remain as some kind of potential for a rainy day. They were meant to be used, to be invested carefully and wisely. The master did not tell the servants how to do this. The freedom, discretion and personal integrity of the servants was respected. We are not puppets on a string, we are given enormous freedom to respond to God's grace and use the talents we have been given.

Back to the story. The man who was given five talents went out immediately and put these talents to work. He was aggressive and self-confident. He would have succeeded in almost any endeavor. Soon the talents had doubled, so that he now had ten talents, an admirable return on his investment. The servant who had been given two talents did much the same thing, he demonstrated discerning wisdom, and soon his two talents had become four. The master was more than pleased with the performance of these two servants, they were given the keys to the kingdom.

Then the tragic dimension of the story unfolds in the report of the third servant. Here was a person filled with fear and timidity. In the back of his mind was a terrible premonition that somehow he might lose his talent. Investing it required risk, and risk was too threatening. Thus, the talent was buried in the ground and wasted. The master is appalled. The servant is disgraced. The talent is misused.

What does this story mean for us? How do we understand Jesus' words and message for today? Three possible implications flow our from this parable.

Five-Opportunity People

To begin, I am assuming that most who read this book, or who are a part of the Christian community today, are five-talent people. Serving in ministry for almost twenty years, I am convinced that our churches are filled with highly talented, gifted, intelligent, discerning, faithful servants. I am in awe much of the time because of the talent, ability and commitment of so many people we serve. Many church leaders seem to believe that they are dealing with primarily one-talent people: however, that is completely foreign to my own experience.

Another assumption. The word "talent" often has become a stumbling block for us. It seems to be a static concept, simply a potential buried deep inside of us, not connected with real life. For the sake of discussion, I would prefer to translate the word "talent" into the word "opportunity". In other words, every one of us, as we travel through life, has been given a multitude of opportunities, of possibilities, more than we could ever imagine.

Time and again the doors have been flung wide open for us, often without any effort or push on our part. An opportunity is different from a talent because it demands that we walk through the doors, that we act, that we respond if the opportune moment is to be seized and become a reality. To pursue opportunities means that life has a sense of movement and challenge and newness. The Master has given each of us magnificent opportunities and has told us to invest ourselves in their pursuit.

Concentrating on the closed doors in life sometimes becomes an obsession. Focus can easily be riveted on problems or roadblocks that loom so forbiddingly. But the parable of Jesus is meant to encourage us to look for the open doors, to realize that no matter how many times the door has been slammed in our face, no matter how many times we have wandered along dead-end roads, countless opportunities still wait for us.

I talked recently with a young woman who just graduated from college. I expected her to give me a litany of problems in her search for a job. Instead she proclaimed that she is literally standing on tiptoe because of all the opportunities which are present. "There are so many doors which are swinging wide open," she told me, "that I hardly can decide what to pursue." She sees all of life as a series of opportunities, and with that kind of fortitude and zeal, there is no telling what she can do with her considerable ability.

This woman's name is Dee. I first met her after she went through a very painful divorce. She told me she was convinced that life was not over for her, that there were many opportunities available, and that she could hardly wait to see what God had in store for her.

Not long after our conversation, our church decided to begin a program entitled "Starting Over Single", a series of seminars for those who had been divorced. Dee volunteered to become a part of the planning group for such an effort. It was an amazing process, a time when Dee and several others worked for months to create an effective program.

As the time approached for the initial seminar, publicity was drafted and sent to the community. We hoped that we would attract at least twenty-five people. This would launch the series on a positive note, but we thought that twenty-five people might be wildly optimistic. However, the first evening 110 people showed up. Dee became one of the speakers for this ministry and took over the training of the group leaders. She had certainly pursued an opportunity, invested herself wisely.

Some months later Dee came to me again and said that she believed God had something more in store for her, that there were new opportunities out there. She asked that we remember her in our prayers. Not long afterwards, our congregation voted to send several people to St. Louis, Missouri, to be trained as leaders in the Stephen Ministry. The Stephen program is a ministry in which congregational members are trained and equipped to be caregivers and compassionate friends to others.

Dee volunteered to be one of the leaders of this new ministry and went to St. Louis for the training. Upon returning, she and her fellow leaders trained thirty of our members in ministry, spending two years with them in intensive instruction and supervision. Each of these trained Stephen Ministers is equipped to provide support, understanding and love to people in need.

Some time later Dee came to see me again, and again she believed that God had some new opportunities for her to pursue. Shortly thereafter, we created a new position on our staff for a person to work with singles and also to coordinate the Stephen

Ministry. Dee applied for that position and was chosen to join our staff. She has helped create a hope-giving ministry for those in need. We all can pursue many opportunities. God opens doors throughout our lives: we need to watch and to walk through these doors.

It would have been easy for Dee, and it is easy for us, to give up, to become discouraged, and to no longer see opportunities. Especially after the event of a tragedy—the death of a marriage, the loss of a job, the loss of a loved one—we sometimes wonder if it is even worth continuing. But God gives us countless opportunities to start over.

Two of the most inspirational people I have ever met are Bill and Sigrid, longtime members of our congregation. They are both five-talent people, in many ways the very fiber and backbone of this community of faith. Some time ago Bill discovered that he has MS, and, although he was able to keep it under control for some years, there was much fear and anxiety about the future.

In recent years, Bill's health has been deteriorating. Walking is no longer possible, and the motorized cart is now a standard part of his life. Other physical liabilities and handicaps face him everday: his life is filled with hardships.

Shortly after Bill learned of his illness, Sigrid discovered that she had lupus. Lupus is another serious illness, affecting the immune system. Sigrid has had to endure a great amount of medication, particularly cortisone, which oftentimes does as much harm to the body as it does good. There has been more physical trials for Sigrid than any of us know.

Yet Bill and Sigrid have absolutely amazed everyone, raising three five-talented daughters, being intensely active in the life of the church. Bill served as president of the congregation, chairman of the personnel committee, a leader in a special fund drive. Even though his body is often weak and unpredictable, Bill's spirit is undeterred, and his mind is sharp and clear. He's at work every day.

Sigrid is the consummate volunteer. She fashions beautiful banners for our sanctuary, serves as a Stephen Minister to those in need, volunteers in the office, and helps with education. The list goes on endlessly. Sigrid has a spirit of joy so contagious that it is caught by everyone around her.

For Bill and Sigrid, life has always been a series of opportunities. When the doors of physical health slammed shut, they found new doors. They have learned that nothing can ever separate us from the love of God in Christ Jesus, nothing can ever take these opportunities away from us. God has given us gifts and talents and has told us to use them. What a joy it is to see people using these opportunities! It makes you want to shout with the Master in the parable, "Well done, share my happiness!"

Money is a Talent

In addition to including the dynamic meaning of "opportunity" whithin it, the word "talent" in the parable of Jesus also has a financial dimension. When we talk about this story, or hear sermons preached on it, we don't very often consider the monetary aspect of the story. It definitely is present. In fact, at the bottom of the page in the Bible where this story is written, there is an asterisk next to the word "talent". The comment is fascinating, it tells us that a talent was worth more than fifteen years' wages of a laborer of the first century. A talent was worth fifteen times the average salary of most people in that period of time.

That means that in Jesus' day a talent was worth at least $1000. Thus, the first servant is given at least $5000, the second servant $2000, and the third servant $1000. That is still no small sum, but in that period of time it was a fortune. If the talent was worth fifteen times the wages of a laborer, and we assume today that perhaps an average salary in our land is $20,000, that means that one talent in today's dollars was worth $300,000. Imagine that, each talent is worth almost a third of a million dollars!

The first two men go out and double their investment. In today's dollars, it means the first man was given five talents, which translates into $1,500,000. He immediately goes out and turns this into 3 million, The second man is given the equivalent of $600,000. He invest it wisely, so that it becomes $1,200,000. When the Master returns, he is thrilled with the efforts of these two servants and says to them, "Well done, good and faithful servant. You have been faithful over a few things, I will put you in charge of many things. Come and share your master's happiness."

What a strange passage! These servants began with exhorbitant amounts of financial resources, then went right out and doubled their holdings. Surprise of surprises, the master praises them for their prowess. A great deal of money has been made, and the Master is thoroughly pleased, both commending and rewarding the servants.

All of this seems to fly in the face of much of what is written or spoken regarding finances in the Christian community today. We have, by and large, decided that the accumulation of sizable fortunes is somehow evil and against the will of God. Many basically have decided that a person who amasses such resources must have compromised so much that they must be living a faithless existence. And there are certainly a number of Scriptural passages which can lead us to this conclusion.

However, in this story Jesus seems to be saying that it is wise and prudent for those people who have been given the gift of making money to use that gift. Those people who have discovered open doors and opportunities and have been given generous resources and are being told to walk through those doors, to invest the talents wisely and prudently. We sometimes have laid all sorts of guilt trips on people who may have this gift, but there is no such teaching in this story. Rather, the parable seems to suggest that the master is thrilled with the accomplishments of his servants.

The talents came from the Master, and they remained the Master's. We can imagine, too, that if the story had continued, we would have seen the fist two servants giving joyfully to others, in response to what their Master had done for them.

Perhaps, just perhaps, this story says that there are some among us who have been given the gift, the talent, the opportunity to multiply their financial resources. This is not a greater gift than any other, but it is a gift, and this gift is meant to be used for the glory of God, as are all the other gifts.

Obviously we must say this with a sense of extreme caution, because there are many pitfalls that line the streets when we talk about wealth. But the parable does lead us to believe that a person who doubles a financial investment, who earns more return in the resources, is using the gift in a wise and discerning manner, as long as it's not done for purely selfish reasons. A great deal of scriptural maturity is necessary when we are handling this kind of a gift, but it is possible to do. This seems to be one lesson from the story.

A congregation in our metropolitan community has run out of room. Several thousand people come to worship on Sunday, and the building simply cannot handle the crowds anymore. The church needs all kinds of space—worship, education, meeting, office, parking. No matter how much a congregation may wish to focus only on the people rather than on bricks and mortar, there are times when consideration of new facilities is essential. People cannot be served if there is not enough space for seating or parking spaces or for education. This congregation was out of room and was now implementing a plan to expand.

A five-million dollar building drive was conceived and accepted by the congregation. Many in the parish believed this was far beyond their capacity. There was too much blue sky in the planning process. The first segment of the fundraising seemed to confirm the skepticism, as only a fraction of the goal was reached.

Suddenly, to the surprise of all, a rather miraculous event took place. One family in the congregation made a commitment of a million dollars to the building fund drive! That kind of giving is almost unheard of in local settings; it only seems to happen somewhere else. Following very quickly after this first commitment, the church then received two other pledges for half a million each, plus one more for a quarter of a million dollars.

Just imagine, four families have made commitments of two-and-one-quarter million dollars! Since that absolutely surprising turn of events, the rest of the money was pledged in short order. The congregation went well over its goal. In addition to the building, some large gifts were designated for benevolence needs elsewhere.

I am continually amazed when I see the amount of money some people have the ability and the opportunity to earn. I am continually astounded as well to see the amount some of these same people will give. For those who have the talent of making huge sums of money, there should be recognition, as in the parable of Jesus, that this is a legitimate talent. However, these same people should also be challenged to see how much of this money they can give away. True worth is not measured in how much we have but in how much we give away.

As in the parable, the talents, the gifts, come from God and He asks for an accounting of them, not only to the wealthy, but to each of us. We are called to generosity, to secrifice, to Biblical stewardship. One of the leaders of the five million-dollar fund drive was an elderly widow, living on social security. At the appointed hour, she was asked to speak in front of the congregation about her giving.

She said to the people, "I have been tithing for the past twenty years, giving ten percent. When my husband died, I did not think I could continue to give like this, but I have been able to keep my tithe current. Right now I am giving about a thousand dollars to the mission of Jesus Christ this year, and I hope I can give even more. Giving is one of the great joys of my life." Most of us are given the talent to earn financial resources and to use that gift to the glory of God.

Five-Talent People Face Adversity Too

I believe that Jesus told this story in order to directly impact people like you and me. We are five-talent people, called by God to use our gifts to the glory of God. For most of us the temptation is to procrastinate, to put it off, to wait for another day to respond. Someday will be a better time than the present. Someday we will have the time and energy. Right now we are faced with this crisis or that hurt or this financial strain. Sometime in the future will be much better.

A common misconception that many of us have is that the most obvious five-talent people in our observation basically have nothing but clear sailing. Adversity skirts around them. They have a teflon coating which does not allow sorrow or pain to stick. We begin to believe that if only we had the kind of open-door existence these people have, then life would be dramatically different for us. We can even complain, "Why do others get all the breaks?

However, I think if we looked closer we would find that very often the people who seem to contain and to use the most talent and the most ability are those who have often shouldered some of the heaviest burdens. Those who have been in the deepest valley have climbed the highest mountain.

Recently there was an article in our local paper about two people hamed Herb and Corrine. Herb is a bishop in the church; his wife, Corrine, is now a pastor at a congregation in our city. Obviously, they are very talented and gifted people. Herb has a Ph.D., has authored books, and both Herb and Corrine are much in demand as speakers and leaders.

Just about a year ago, their 18 year old son, Andrew, then a freshman in college, committed suicide in the basement of their home. It was a devastating and shocking experience. Then a few months later, a pastor who was mentally unbalanced threatened

Herb's life and showed up in Herb's office appearing to have a gun in his pocket. Shortly thereafter, Herb discovered that he had cancer of the prostate. Surgery has apparently cured the illness, but it has been a difficult and trying year.

It would have been easy for them to retreat into a shell, to hide away in an expression of self-pity or defeat. Any kind of risk might have been seen as too painful. Corrine and Herb, however, are not the kind who run away and hide, but rather, who see opportunities as gifts and see themselves as stewards of their many talents.

Paraphrasing Corrine, "I feel a greater surge of life now. I have a deeper appreciation of life. I feel as if I have experienced the worst pain of my life. But somehow, the resurrection power I am experiencing shows me that whatever I face, it won't be worse than this."

Herb added these words, "I am more courageous now. When you look death in the face, other things don't seem as frightening. I have a courage about life."

Corrine responded, "I give myself more now to help other people. I know how important it is to rally a community of hope in a time of crisis. I feel a strong surge of courage I didn't know before. I don't wait to get better. I'm surprised at the new courage. I feel a part of eternity in a way I didn't feel before."

We all have the opportunity to be five-talent people, just like Herb and Corrine. Resources and opportunities abound for each of us at every period of life. Sometimes, even though these gifts appear all around us, these gifts remain unnoticed, unused. What are some of the most obvious gifts?

Six Gifts

We have been given the gift of **life.** If God had not given us this unique gift, there would be no others. Incorporated into this gift of life are our bodies, our minds and our spirits. God has given to us infinite value—we are not machines or computers, not like the dust which the wind blows away. We are flesh and blood and spirit and life. The Psalmist describes this creation, "We are fearfully and wonderfully made." In the midst of this created self we are given maximum opportunities for good, for growth, for talent for leadership for creativity. God's creation in the gift of birth and of life stands supreme.

We are given the gift of **rebirth.** In Baptism, God gives us the grace-full gift of a new life, life in Jesus Christ, life in the power of the Holy Spirit, life as children of the Father. Baptism continues to remind us that we are never alone in this lonely world. We are children of the King, a part of the family of God. No matter what the power of darkness might be around us, we are a part of the light. We are reborn, born of the water and of the spirit. Baptism is an eternal gift.

We are given the gift of a **family.** We do not emerge from a test tube to be released into a cold, cruel world. We are born into a family. Almost all of us have been given the amazing warmth and love of a family, or whoever nurtured and cared for us—parents and grandparents, brothers and sisters, aunts and uncles.

The family has imparted to us our very first truths about God, about the gifts we were given, about our own value and worth. Within that family we were challenged to develop many of our gifts, gifts of speech and hearing, of walking and running, of reading and loving. The family gave us a name, a status, a self-image, a self-understanding, a sense of acceptance. What a magnificent gift!

We are given the gift of the **church,** the body of Christ. The church is not always what it was meant to be. Sometimes it reeks with prejudice, pettiness and irrelevancy. the world shouts at us from every direction, "Buy this, do this, eat that, drink this. Then you will find meaning." But in the church we are reminded that only in the Christian Gospel can true meaning be found.

In Jesus Christ, in the cross on Calvary is the message of life, that we have a reason to live and we have a hope when we die. We are reminded each week as we worship that we are not alone, that there are so many others around the world who stand with us in prayer and in worship, in celebration and hope. No matter what may fall apart in our lives, in the church we can see the message of salvation and the love of the Christian family. Jesus gave us the gift of the church so that we might find an unmovable anchor in a world which is constatnly shifting.

We are given the gift of our **individuality,** our personhood. No matter how insignificant we might feel much of the time, the Bible tells us that we are absolutly unique, created in the image of God. We have not been stamped out on a press, but created "a little lower than the angels." Everyone of us has been given this same gift, the special qualities of personality, talent, and imagination. In addition, when Christ lives within us, we have a spirit of love and joy and care for others which is clearly visible. God created each of us as we are, with a unique sparkle and shine, so that we might let others see his reflection in us. We have the gift of our uniqueness. God wants you to be you and me to be me.

We are given the gift of **compassion.** Within each of us has been placed the heart of Jesus Christ. We may not always belive that it is present; we may try to bury it, but that heart is there. From His heart pulses life, giving love and compassion. When others hurt, we hurt; when others find life to be falling apart, we are able to stand with them.

A world without compassion is like the earth without sunshine. We love because he first loved us. "So faith, hope, love abide, these three; but the greatest of these is love." I Corinthians 13:13. We have been given the gift of compassion, propelling us to carry out the visit, to make the phone call, to send the love note, to say the prayer on behalf of another, to give the hug to one who is feeling empty and sad. Not one of us has been excluded from receiving this gift of compassion. such beauty can emanate from each of us.

In summary, gifts are everywhere. God has placed them within us and surround us. He wants us to use them, for our sake and for others. Individually we are filled with talents. As congregations, the giftedness is overwhelming. Think for a moment of a few gifts which are present.

A Basketful of Gifts

—There are some who have the gift of working with their hands, of creating masterpieces out of wood or metal or cloth—use that gift to the glory of God!

—There are some who have the gift of organization, who can take project from the beginning and carry it out all the way to the end—use that gift to the glory of God!

—There are some who have the gift of making money, who can take five dollars and make ten, or one hundred, who have the magic quality of investing wisely—use that gift to the glory of God!

—There are some who have the gift of loving little children who can create a special bond with these little ones and share God's love with them—use that gift to the glory of God!

—There are some who have mastered the intricacies of new technology, who know how to use computers to open up wonderful new vistas of knowledge and communication—use that gift to the glory of God!

—There are some who have the gift of teaching, who can motivate students to develop a real love for learning—use that gift to the glory of God!

—There are some who have the gift of music, who have a talent for finding this harmony in God's creation—use that gift to the glory of God!

—There are some who have the gift of writing, a remarkable talent for taking ideas, feelings, and stories and placing them on the printed page—use that gift to the glory of God!

—There are some who have the gift of mechanics, who can fix anything, who can unscramble the complexities of modern engines or machines—use that gift to the glory of God!

—There are some who have the gift of medicine, who can provide healing and wholeness to those who are suffering—use that gift to the glory of God!

—There are some who have the gift of gardening, who can take a yard or a garden or a field and make it blossom with beauty and produce—use that gift to the glory of God!

—There are some who have the gift of working with the forgotten of our world in nursing homes, in prison, or with those who have been battered or bruised—use that gift to the glory of God!

—There are some who have the gift of management, of helping others to utilize their gifts—use that gift to the glory of God!

—There are some who have the gift of selling, of understanding what others want or need, of meeting the needs of those whom they serve—use that gift to the glory of God!

The list could be almost endless. Whatever gift you have been given, use the gift! Give thanks for the gift, develop the gift, invest it wisely in this world, and do all to the glory of God!

Three men in the parable of the talents were given gifts. Two of them multiplied the gifts and were commended by the master. The other buried the gift in the ground. clearly we see which of these examples we are called to follow.

Chapter Four

LET ME TELL YOU A STORY

A PASSION FOR EXCELLENCE

The Kingdom of heaven. Such an impressive reality. When you talk about a Kingdom, it immediately conjures an image of something grand and glorious, something regal and awesome. Jesus talked a great deal about the Kingdom. It was one of the favorite topics of discussion among all those who followed. I am sure that day after day came the request, "Jesus, tell us about the kingdom. Describe heaven! Let us catch a glimpse of some of these secrets of the universe."

Jesus describes the heavenly Kingdom as more than a place. In fact, the kingdom is depicted more in terms of an action verb rather than a noun. It is the kingly rule of God. We do not have to wait until some future life to experience the Kingdom of heaven; it is a reality present at this very moment. Because the Kingdom is already present, everything about this world and about our lives changes. The kingdom is both now and not yet, it is here and yet it will arrive in the future, it is finished but not yet finished. Jesus brought the kingdom into being, yet it is still in the process of coming.

The late Dr. Kent Knutson once used an instance which had happened with his son to describe the kingdom. Christmas presents had been purchased and were hidden in the attic of their home. Before leaving for a few hours, the Knutsons told their son not to go looking for his present. He should wait until Christmas.

As soon as the parents returned home, however, they could tell that their son had caught a glimpse of this gift. It was written all over his face. He had seen the gift that was to come, he had a foretaste of that reality, but it was not yet his completely. We are part of the kingdom of heaven right now, but we have not received it yet in all of its fullness.

Jesus could have spent much of his time defining the kingdom of heaven. Analysis and definition are often a very worthwhile enterprise. The problem is, few are usually listening. Instead, Jesus told stories and most everyone listened. The kingdom is portrayed from many different vantage points, kind of like viewing a diamond from every conceivable side. Parables are especially effective in giving us this opportunity to take a number of various sightings.

Matthew 13 is full of "mini" stories about the kingdom of heaven. Jesus begins one passage after another with the words, "The kingdom of heaven is like...," as he paints a new picture. The kingdom is like a mustard seed, like yeast, like sowing seed in a field, like a treasure hidden in a field, like a net dropped into the lake to catch fish. Once again Jesus says to his followers as they press him about the kingdom, "Let me tell you a story."

Matthew 13:45-46. "Again the kingdom of heaven is like a merchant looking for fine pearls. When he found one of great value, he went away and sold everything that he had and bought it."

In other words, Jesus is saying, if you want to know what the kingdom of heaven is like, it is like a person who is on a lifelong search for that which is excellent. The man in the story is trying to find the most priceless and invaluable pearl one could possibly discover, and when he finds it, he will sell everything that he has in order to purchase the gem. Unquestionably, this is the driving force in his life, to find the pearl and then to possess it as his own. This, Jesus says, is what the kingdom of heaven is like.

The value of the pearl of excellence is infinite and its possession so crucial that it is worth spending our entire lives in pursuit. We are called to give ourselves the highest, the most valuable, the most precious. To invest oneself in anything less valuable, to spend a lifetime pursuing that which is inferior would not only be a waste but also a tragedy. Our lives have such value and purpose that we should search unendingly and tirelessly for the best, for that which is good and acceptable and perfect.

Jesus rephrases this story in the Sermon on the Mount. "But seek first his kingdom and his righteousness, and all these things will be given to you as well." Matthew 6:35. To be under the kingly rule of God is to constantly search for that which is above everything else. The Apostle Paul writes in Colossians, "Set your minds on that which is above." Col 3:2. Search for the best, the most excellent pearl.

Magnificent Psalm 8 carves out another description of the infinite value of human life. You and I have been created in the image of God: in fact, we have been created "a little lower than the angels." Psalms 8:5. Other translations declare that we have been created a little less than God, and crowned with glory and honor. Imagine that, created a little less than God and crowned with glory and honor! How can we then be satisfied with anything less than excellence!

One of the favorite hymns in Christendom is entitled "Amazing Grace". In the first stanza we find the words, "Amazing Grace, how sweet the sound, that saved a wretch like me." What an erroneous set of words. We are not wretches, we are not worms, we are not worthless creatures. Some of our behavior may be wretched at times, but we are not wretches! Rather, we need to be reminded by the Psalmist that we are created in the image of God, crowned with glory and honor, a little lower than the angels.

Since the value of our lives is beyond measurement, we are to spend them in pursuit of only the best. Our talents and abilities are to be directed at a search for excellence. We are to be all that we can be: we are to use all of the gifts we have been given. Life is meant to be a relentless search for that which is most precious, like a pearl.

A professor I had at the seminary challenged all of us when we were seniors to spend our lives in the pursuit of excellence. He suggested that each of us find an area of our work or ministry in which we could develop a special expertise. This could be some area of study, some kind of special ministry—youth, education, counseling, preaching, visiting, etc.—or it could be in some additional field such as writing, public speaking, or administration.

We cannot be good at everything, but we need to discover our God-given gifts. This is one of the reasons why I have discovered the gift of writing books. I hope to continue to develop expertise and effectiveness in this area. I may be a lousy singer, and I can't fix anything on my automobile, but I can put one word after another on the printed page. We are called to search in our own lives for that which is excellent.

Christians often are confused about the relationship between humility and servanthood. In seeking to take the lowest place, as Jesus suggests in another story, in trying to be content and to spend our lives in service, life has sometimes become a time of trivial pursuits. We talk ourselves into believing that if we settle for the mundane, the passionless existence, then we are following the will of God for us. At the same time, if we do search for that which is an excellent piece of the full and abundant life, then we sometimes believe we are not sufficiently humble. But to be humble, to keep a sense of humor about oneself, to live in a state of forgiveness, does not preclude the search for excellence.

The same problem often happens in congregations. A parish may be fading into the background; it may be declining in every area. Some people interpret this as being evidence that they are truly faithful to the Gospel. We often hear the words, "We are called to be faithful, not to be successful." But faithfulness does not mean passivity; holiness does not have to be synonomous with mediocrity.

In fact, there is nothing in the Scriptures which baptizes failure, which gives us the green light to spend our lives on behalf of mediocrity and blandness. Instead Jesus says, "The kingdom of heaven is like the search for a pearl of great price." It is to have a passion for excellence. Remember the pearl!

A few years ago, Tom Peters and Robert Waterman wrote a book that became a best seller; the title was *In Search of Excellence.* The subject material had to do primarily with the business world, yet much of the book could have applied to the local congregation, as well as to our individual lives. *"In Search of Excellence"* is not a bad theme for any of us to follow. Surely it would characterize the search of the person for the pearl.

More recently, Tom Peters has joined with Nancy Austin to write another book which was titled, *A Passion for Excellence. A Passion for Excellence.* I am intrigued by the title. The book itself is hard to follow and at times is too technical for many, but the title gives pause for reflection. What is communicated to me is that excellence is not a by-product, not an add-on, and not just a side benefit that comes when everything is done well.

Rather, excellence becomes the primary focus of life. Such a driving force is the conviction that if something is worth doing at all, it is worth doing well. I remember Professor Arndt Halvorson from Luther-Northwestern Seminary telling a story about his father, a man who spent his whole working life as a craftsman. One day Arndt asked his father why he had devoted his life to working with his hands, to building, to creating.

His father answered, "I find working with wood irrestible. To fashion something out of wood with my own two hands is the greatest challenge and gives me the greatest reward in this life." He grasped the pursuit of excellence; he understood about the pearl of great price. We discover our gifts and then use them in as excellent a manner as possible.

Peters and Austin describe this passion for excellence in the following way, "The pursuit of excellence is not for the faint of heart. It is most often achieved by people who muster up the nerve and the passion to step out, in spite of doubt or fear. And the center of this passion is a great deal of courage and self-respect, as well as tenacity. It is hanging in there long after others have given up."

Then the key sentences, "It means that anything else than your best really bothers you, maybe even keeps you awake at night. The passion for excellence opens you up to criticism, disappointment, disillusionment, and failure. But the passionate, courageous and self-respecting people cannot wait to face challenges or risks. Many people see mountains as great obstacles. The person who has a passion for excellence sees that same mountain as something to be climbed or else."

These words remind us of Jesus' story of the mustard seed. "If you have faith as a mustard seed, you will be able to say to the mountain, 'Move hence to yonder place,' and it will move, and nothing will be impossible for you." Matthew 17:20. Jesus spent a great deal of time talking about the passion for excellence, which comes by yielding our lives to His power while using different language to do so. Many of his stories are pictures of excellence. Life is meant to be spent in searching for the most precious, the highest, the most valuable pearl.

In the Sermon the on Mount, Jesus declared to each of us, "You are the light of the world, you are the salt of the earth." Matthew 5:13, 14. In other words, you have been given amazing talents and abilities, you have been given the power of the Holy spirit. I expect you to pursue that which is excellent. I have called you to be among those who will change the world, who will bring about the kingdom of God, who will stand up for what is good and excellent and perfect.

Consider with me four different facets of this search.

Goals

To have a passion for excellence means that we develop the right goals in life. Many people aim at nothing and hit it every time. If we don't know where we are going, any road will take us there. It is imperative that we set our eyes on the true goals before we launch out into the deep.

Jesus said, "Seek first the kingdom of God." Matthew 6:32. Paul writes, "Do everything in the name of the Lord Jesus." Colossians 3:17. The goal of our lives should be to lift high the cross, to share the love of Jesus Christ with the entire world. It means that we must use all of our gifts and talents for the glory of God.

The Biblical principle touches each one of us. The school teacher strives to be an excellent teacher, challenging students to lift their sights ever higher. Our daughter finished her senior year in high school recently, and she had some absolutely brilliant teachers. She was challenged and her sights were lifted far more than we ever could have expected. What a difference it has made for her and for her fellow students that these teachers live with a passion for excellence, both for themselves and for their students.

Gospel-giving goals means that each individual has a passion for excellence—the business-person, the farmer, the engineer, the pilot, the nurse, the builder, the homemaker, the pastor, the programmer, the doctor, every one of us is called to a pursuit of the excellent pearl.

I have a friend who is an auto mechanic in a large garage. He is consistently working for excellence, working harder and more diligently than most of the other workers. This has been a source of tension among some other mechanics. They do not like to see excellence in one of their peers. They would prefer to avoid this kind of pressure.

Recently an opportunity came for my friend to receive training in a new area of auto mechanics, something to do with computers in the cars. He applied to go to school for this special area of work. But some of the other mechanics campaigned against this. They knew that if he were trained in this area he would immediately work much harder and more effectively than they. Such an example would not be good for their standing in the company. People with a passion for excellence often threaten those around them.

Sometimes the world pushes us to change our goals, to settle for second best, to pursue the pearl of little value. Jesus was constantly prodded and challenged to pursue a different route to accomplish his goals. Mary begged him, "Jesus, you don't have to really die, why not become a political savior?"

In the graphic story of the devil tempting Jesus in Matthew 4:1-11, the devil challenges Jesus to go for the spectacular, to jump off of the pinacle of the temple, to win the world, not through the cross, but through a coronation. But Jesus replied to this tempatation, "Get behind me Satan."

There are always temptations that come our way to knock us off course. The Apostle Paul says it best as he introduces his magnificent 13th chapter of First Corinthians, "Let me show you a still more excellent way, the way of love." Each of us needs to set our face toward the goal of the excellent pearl, the highest and the best in life. Search for the kingdom of God. Don't let anyone push you off course!

Learning from the Past

To have a passion for excellence means to learn from the past. I am sure that the merchant who finally possessed the pearl of great value had gone down many dead end roads. He had many heartaches and disappointments during his search. But he learned from his experience and found new ways to discover his goal.

We must admit that we stumble and fall very often. We get sidetracked so easily and waste much of our time, energy and money on the side roads. That's why we need to live each day in confession and forgiveness. We need to confess that we often have not searched for excellence, but have spent our lives in the pits. To find a more excellent and fulfilling life is to be willing to admit our sin, our mistakes, and to learn from them as we continue to search for excellence.

A professional football coach in our community took over the team as a relatively young man, still in his 30's. This was his first head coaching job. Clearly he was an unknown quantity to everyone, probably even to himself. The season turned out to be a disaster for all, including the coach, and he was terminated from his position at the end of the season.

After the situation had calmed a bit, after the storm had settled, this newly unemployed coach was interviewed and asked to comment about the past year. One of the questions had to do with what he had learned from his year as a head coach. What would he change if he were to do it over again? Most of us can understand this. After our first year in any new situation, we can look back and see much that we would like to change and improve, and new directions we could pursue.

The answer of this coach went like this, "I wouldn't change much of anything. I think we were on the right track all the way down the line. I would do it all the same way again." To me, that answer doesn't have the ring of a productive pursuit of excellence. It seems the coach didn't learn anything from the past year's failures. To reach for excellence, it is incumbent that a person learn from the past and then discover changes for the future.

I believe a more appropriate response would have gone something like this, "Well, I made some mistakes this year, I tried some new things which just didn't work out. I have learned a great deal from this experience, and I would certainly be a much wiser coach and do things differently if I were to do it again." The person searching for the pearl of great price must be willing to confess and be forgiven, to learn from past failures, to listen to others, to be willing to start afresh. Confession, absolution, and then a new beginning.

A humorist has said that the reason golf is such a popular sport is that it gives you eighteen chances to start over agin. To be forgiven means starting all over again, learning from the past, and then moving on.

Another example comes from the corporate world. There is a birth control device that proved to be one of the great success stories in the national health care industry for some years. It was seen as a safe alternative to the pill. But it suddenly became apparent that this device was very dangerous. It caused infection, infertility, unwanted abortions, and even in some cases, death.

A federal judge lectured the company in no uncertain terms, "Your company caused injuries by the thousands. And when the time came for these women to make their claims against your company, you attacked their characters ... You have taken the bottom line as your guiding beacon and the low road as your route. This is corporate irresponsibility at its meanest."

Shortly after the judges diatribe, the president of the company which had manufactured these devices said, in effect, that he was still proud of the device. It had done so much good for so many. The only problem in this event was that we are now living in a society where people sue at the drop of a hat. As far as doing anything different in his company in the future, the answer was no. In the Presidents' opinion there was no lesson to be learned from this tragedy.

Such a defense is astounding. The only person who can truly search for excellence is the one who admits sinfulness, who confesses mistakes and errors. Once we have done this, once we have learned from the past, once we have started over, then we can continue our pursuit of excellence.

Possibilities

A person committed to a passion for excellence is one who truly believes that possessing the pearl of great price is possible in this life. There is a profound conviction that this abundance and excellence can be found. Sometimes we're apt to be caught up in a spirit of cynicism and despair, to pessimistically adopt the attitude that life in only a series of dead ends, or that we somehow missed the lineup the day that talents and abilities were passed out. Life can be a continuous process of putting ourselves down, of believing that excellence and value have certainly eluded us.

We need to hear again the words of the Apostle Paul, "I can do all things through Christ who strengthens me." Philippians 4:13. With God all things are possible. We need to believe that excellence is possible for us, that the opportunity to search for the highest and the best is ours. Above all, we need to hear again that all of this does not happen on our own, by our own reason or strength, but that God works through us and in us.

A teenage boy planned a ball game in his back yard. Only one problem stood in the way. In fact it was an ever-present obstacle present when some event was proposed for the yard. Right in the middle of the lawn was a large boulder. Sometimes the rock had been used as second base, and other times as home plate, depending on which direction the game was played. Still, it was always frustratingly in the way.

On this particular day, the boy decided to move the stone. His muscles were developing. He had been lifting a few weights, he had the first evidences of whiskers on his upper lip, and his voice was growing deeper. Why not move that boulder!

He took a powerful stance next to the stone, flexed his muscles, put his shoulder directly against it, and pushed with all of his might. Nothing happened! He tried again with the same result. Walking around to the other side of this monumental opponent, he tried still another time. Nothing! The boulder was simply too much for him.

At that moment he saw a two-by--four lying nearby, so he decided to use it as a kind of a wedge. Putting it under one side, he was able to get the rock to move, to wiggle a bit, even to rise ever so slightly off the ground. But while he was holding the board, he couldn't reach the boulder to push it, and in the end it wouldn't budge.

At that moment he became conscious of someone watching him, and looking up he saw his father standing there. He had no idea how long had had been in the yard. After a few awkward moments, his father said to him, "I don't think you have been using all of the strength that you have at your disposal, you have more power available than what you have been using."

The boy became angry. "What do you mean, I have been pushing as hard as I can, I have been using every ounce of muscle that I have. That rock will never move. It's hopeless."

"No," said his father, "you haven't used all of your strength. I have been standing here for some time now and you haven't asked me to help you. Together we should be able to move that boulder."

Amazing potential appears for us when we use and rely on all of our God-given power and strength. Jesus says that we can do all that he has done; if fact, we will do greater things that he has done, even move mountains. Never underestimate what we can do in Jesus' name.

Peters and Austin, in the book *The Passion for Excellence,* make one further point. They cite a study from the Duke University Medical Center in which a scientist in his work exploring Type A personalities (those hard driving, impatient, relentless folks who are thought to be more prone to heart attacks) found that one element stood out more than any other as a serious problem.

This element was cynicism. It was discovered that cynicism is the most toxic ingredient in the entire body. The more a person is beset by cynicism, or self-doubt, or just plain apathy, the less chance there is to find that precious pearl.

The authors conclude that the passion for excellence is predictable in someone with an optimistic attitude, a belief that life has value, that life is worth an all-out effort. I paraphrase a summary of their findings, "When a person has a true passion for excellence, they will stand straighter, look people in the eye, see things as they actually are, and walk with a spring in their step. For they have something to deeply care about, and to which they can commit themselves. It is the healthiest way to live."

Jesus lived with a passion for excellence. The parables he taught were crafted with beautiful imagery and powerful meaning. The way he reached out to the sick and the needy packs a mountain of meaning for the way we are to live. His care and encouragement to the disciples and other followers was often painstakingly difficult and all-consuming, but he knew it was worth the effort. In teaching them about a passion for excellence, in giving them the resources neccessary, he provided a foundation for us all.

Jesus took the highest road no matter where it led, even when it ended on a cross. It was on the cross that the kingdom of heaven was most clearly presented, where the pearl of great price was offered to each of us.

Philippians 2:7-11 says, "He made himself nothing, taking the very nature of a servant, being made in human likeness. And being found in appearance as a man, he humbled himself and became obedient to death, even death on a cross! Therefore God exalted him to the highest place and gave him the name that is above every name, that at the name of Jesus every knee should bow in heaven and on earth and under the earth, and every tongue confess that Jesus Christ is Lord, to the glory of God the Father."

The cross became a still more excellent way. Jesus is exalted and glorified. Whenever we follow the more excellent way that God has for us then we too find the glory of His kingdom for us.

Sharing the Pearl

Jesus also taught that it is imperative to share the pearl of excellence and abundance with others. If the man who found the precious pearl would have taken it and entombed it in a bank vault, only taking it out once in a while for his own personal gratification, then he would have missed the whole point of Jesus' words. This passion for excellence is meant to be shared on behalf of others in our world.

One way we can do this is to share our own gifts and talents with those around us. I find it most exciting to spend time with people who have developed a true passion for excellence. I want to share their insights and discoveries. This may be another pastor, a business person, a school teacher, a missionary, an athlete, a craftsman, a writer —the list is endless. I am truly inspired when I am in the presence of one who has committed his or her life to the pursuit of excellence.

I have a good friend who is a pastor of a large congregation nearby. His leadership is dynamic and perceptive and demonstrates excellence. I call him often, seeking his insight and wisdom concerning various areas of congregation life. "What do you do in this situation," I ask him, and, "how have you responded to this need?"

Almost without exception I find that he has already thought through and acted effectively in areas that cause me to struggle. I learn a great deal from him, especially through our conversations, because he has very specifically dedicated himself to a constant search for excellence, to a pursuit of the highest and the best. I think he has discovered the meaning of this parable.

I remember first hearing the story of Mr. LeTourneau many years ago. He was the owner of a heavy equipment company who had discovered the secret of not only making an excellent product, but also of earning huge sums of money. Excellence for him was a goal not just achieved for himself but also for others, so he committed himself to giving 90% of what he earned away. Our first response might be that if we earned that much money, the 10% would still be more than enough on which to live, True, but if it is so easy to give that much away, why aren't more people doing it? He most specifically wanted to share with others.

We are called to share our passion for excellence with others. Those who teach Sunday School are sharing the pearl of faith in

Christ and knowledge of His love with others. Those who are in caring ministries are sharing the gift of excellence through compassion and love.

Whatever we have discovered to be excellence, whatever skills, talents and resources we have been given, we are called to share these unreservedly with others. Like the manna in the Old Testament wilderness, anything which is hoarded will spoil, but that which is given away will bear much excellent fruit.

What about each of us? Have we committed our lives to finding the excellence pearl, the one in this life that is genuinely priceless? There are many pearls which on the surface look all polished and shiny but which are worthless at the core. Don't give up. Find the true pearl of great price!

The kingdom of heaven is like a man who searched for a precious pearl and once having found it, lets nothing on earth prevent him from possessing it. May this be a picture of our lives as well.

THE KINGDOM OF HEAVEN IS LIKE A GREAT BANQUET

Jesus must have loved to eat, but with others, not alone. So many of the stories and events of the Gospels revolve around eating and food that mealtime must have been a pivotal time for him. He seems to have especially loved banquets, parties, wedding celebrations, and picnics. Not surprisingly, the Sacrament of Holy Communion takes place at a meal, where the disciples are eating and drinking. Jesus instructs the disciples to remember him by a meal, that he would continue to be with them.

The fourteenth chapter of Luke is again a story about a dinner, this one taking place at the home of one of the Pharisees. Incidently, there are three stories in this chapter, each one of them about a meal, each about a celebration such as a banquet, each with a profound meaning for the followers of Jesus. The third of these parables is found in Luke 14:16-24, as Jesus turned the moment into a teaching time with the words, "Let me tell you a story.'"

"A certain man was preparing a great banquet and invited many guests. At the time of the banquet he sent his servant to tell those who had been invited. 'Come, for everything is now ready.' But they all alike began to make excuses. The first said, 'I have just bought a field, and I must go and see it. Please excuse me,' Another said, 'I have just bought five yoke of oxen, and I'm on my way to try them out. Please excuse me.'

Still another said, 'I just got married, so I can't come.' The servant came back and reported this to his master. Then the owner of the house became angry and ordered his servant, 'Go out quickly into the streets and alleys of the town and bring in the poor, the crippled, the blind and the lame.'

'Sir,' the servant said, 'what you ordered has been done, but there is still room.' Then the master told his servant, 'Go out to the roads and country lanes and make them come in, so that my house may be full. I tell you, not one of those men who were invited will get a taste of my banquet.' "

I remember that a long time ago when I was in junior high school I wanted in the worst way to be invited to a certain party. There was the feeling deep down inside of me that my entire future was dependent on being included in that elite gathering. Anyone who was anyone in that junior high school would be invited to the party, and I wanted desperately to be a part of that group.

I recall being especially solicitous of those who had control of issuing the invitations, dropping subtle and not-so-subtle hints, hoping that such politicking would bear fruit. But when the invitations were finally sent out, I was not included in the chosen few. Feeling crushed and very unwanted, I found much difficulty in even showing my face in public. School became a terrible ordeal. What if someone would ask me if I were going to the party? What could I say to save some kind of face?

I even manufactured a story suggesting that I had a previous commitment for that evening so that it would have been a physical impossibility for me to join in the festivities. Suddenly, however, a strange phenomenon occurred.

First, one of the more influential kids decided not to go to the party, then another followed suit, then another and another. More than half a dozen or so of the "in" crowd for one reason or another, decided not to attend the celebration. Not surprisingly, the people who were hosting that party were more than a little hurt and upset.

Their response was immediate. I, and some of my other friends, suddenly received an invitation to the party. The people in charge were trying to fill the gaps, and I was to be one of the gap fillers. I debated whether or not I should accept the invitation under such humiliating circumstances. After all, I was only a second choice, only a second-class citizen in the scheme of things. It took me at least thirty seconds to decide that it was better to go under a cloud than not to go at all. To the party I went, and for some imperceptible reason, it had very little to do with my future.

My thoughts and feelings about this party came flooding back to me when I first read this parable of Jesus. The parallel is not absolute, but the banquet has some dynamics in common with my experience. A banquet was, in Jesus' day, a huge celebration where most of the influential people in the community were invited. Clearly this was a gathering for the movers and the shakers, the members of the official or unofficial social registry. All of those who were invited initially agreed to attend.

What is also clear is that the common folk were deliberately excluded, everyday people just like us were not invited. The outcasts and outsiders in the community were not even considered. There was no room in the banquet hall for ordinary people, exactly what happens when royalty, such as Prince Charles and Lady Di visit our country. Most of us are still waiting for our first invitation to a banquet in their honor, and we will no doubt continue to wait for a long time.

As the day for the banquet came near, the unexpected began to happen. Some of the folks who had been invited to the feast decided they were too busy for such a party. They discovered other priorities, and so they bailed out. The excuses were not very original, in fact they were rather lame, but that doesn't seem to matter much to those who no longer wished to attend.

As we might expect, the host preparing the banquet was not at all pleased by this turn of events. All of the weeks and months of planning and execution of this dinner were suddenly thrown into jeopardy. What a disgusting turn of events. Everything is now ready, and suddenly people are not coming. What can be done — the food is prepared, the tables are set, the musicians are hired — yet people are dropping out one after another.

What should he do? Should the whole event be cancelled? Does he throw up his hands and just lock up and go on vacation? Or does he prepare for only a remnant, a much smaller crowd? This host decides to do the unexpected, to embark on a course of action which would be more than a little shocking to the community and to those who were still planning to come to the feast.

Since the banquet is all prepared and there is plenty of room, why not just invite a whole different crowd? So what if this is not the most favored group; who cares if this party will be filled with people who have not hung their hats on a rung of the local social hierarchy. Better that the room be full than worry too much about the status of the people who are attending.

What happened was that the latecomers to the banquet were people who had never been invited before. These were the people judged by the society of that time to be marginal. Some of them were seen as parasites in the community, those who normally remained invisible. The underclass was definitely in evidence at the gala, a radical turn of events for that time or any time in history.

The owner made a conscious decision. If the privileged group would not attend, then he would invite those who never seemed to be invited to such events—the handicapped, the poor, the forgotten, the second and third-class citizens. Perhaps many of these folks were not that much different from us, always hoping to be invited to one of these festive events, but never possessing the needed connections.

The banquet itself must have been near chaos, especially when some of those newly invited folk started arriving. Righteous indignation must have flowed as easily as wine when those from the original list saw who was flooding into the banquet hall. However, they had not seen anything yet, for the banquet hall still offered rows of empty tables and chairs and platters heaped with mountains of magnificent food. All would be wasted unless more people were invited.

Thus the servants were sent out again with more invitations, this time into the countryside. There people were found who were completely on the fringe. Probably some were outlaws, like the kind who attacked people along the roadside, as in the story of the Good Samaritan. Some were shepherds, a group always at the bottom of the social ladder. Some were the homeless, itinerant farmers. Perhaps, (perish the thought) some even were lepers who had been driven out of the city because of their illness. All were invited to the Great Banquet.

What does all of this mean? A strange story! It seems almost incomprehensible to us, looking back from our particular historical vantage point. What an unsettling impact this event would have had on people of that day and age. What a jolt it should also give us. What are its implications?

The Joyous Meal

Jesus pictures the kingdom of God as a banquet, similar to a party, or a celebration. Above all it is meant to be an attitude, a community gathering in thanksgiving, as well as a place or event. Joy, laughter, communion and festivities are to be present. So often we have tended to focus on an image of the kingdom as a rather dull and foreboding place, evoking the same feelings we have when we sit in a formal room attired in stiff and uncomfortable clothing, being forced to endure stale, stifling conversation.

Jesus isn't saying that in this parable; rather he says the Kingdom of God is like a banquet, a feast, a celebration. At times the community of faith indeed becomes very solemn. We never want to minimize the tragedy and reality of evil. But the kingdom overcomes this darkness. It is like a great banquet.

We have a friend who has a picture of Jesus hanging in his living room. Surprisingly, in this picture Jesus is laughing. In fact, it clearly seems as if Jesus is in the midst of a hand-clapping, foot-stomping party, and he has just thrown back his head and let go with a huge belly laugh. How many of us have ever seen a picture like this? I can't even recall another picture of Jesus smiling. Yet a banquet, a wedding feast, and the other gatherings with his closest friends, would all have been heavily seasoned with laughs and smiles.

The most surprising aspect of the picture portraying Jesus laughing was the response of so many people who came to our friend's home. So many people were offended by such an interpretation that the painting was finally placed somewhere out of sight. Our imaginations have difficulty capturing that image of Jesus laughing, filled with joy or smiling. Remember the great feast where people gathered to rejoice, to celebrate, to participate in a kind of holy hilarity. Jesus says in this story that the kingdom of God is like a banquet.

When our family moved to Burnsville, Minnesota, back in 1970, it was a difficult time of transition. We were only across the city from where we used to live, but it seemed as if we were across the country. Of course I went right to work and quickly became immersed in the duties of the church, but my family felt isolated in this new setting. With winter coming, not a lot of opportunity to become a part of the neighborhood or the community presented itself. We often felt alone.

About that time a group of couples who had been meeting together for dinner invited Jackie and me to be a part of that group. Five couples had been meeting, and they thought it would be a good idea to have an even dozen people. Some of the people in this group had been a part of the call committee which had invited us to come to their Burnsville church, so they must have felt some ownership in our adjustment period. They wanted us to feel welcome in this new community, so we joined them for dinner.

What has happened is that we have been gathering together every month or six weeks for fifteen years, joining for dinner at the home of one of the couples. Above all, it has been a celebration. We have had the most festive banquets one could ever imagine. We have sung, ate, and prayed, and laughed and laughed and laughed. Most often the atmosphere bubbles over with joy and hilarious conversation. I believe this is something of a foretaste of the kingdom of God.

Perhaps the closest parallel to the Great Banquet that we as Americans share is the event of Thanksgiving. At this time of the year people gather together with families or close friends to spend a whole day rejoicing. Sometimes it extends into an entire weekend. We give thanks for all of our blessings—we eat, laugh, converse, play and pray together. We embrace each other, just enjoying this time together. Jesus paints a picture of the kingdom of God that looks very much like Thanksgiving—a wonderful feast, a praise-filled event.

The Inclusive Meal

The overwhelming abundance present is a major focus of the Great Banquet. Just as in Thanksgiving, so at the banquet in the story there is always more than any of us could ever imagine or deserve. The overwhelming grace of God shines through. God is always more willing to give than we are to receive. This is not some kind of snack, or some hors d'oeuvre party, this is a banquet with nourishment that never quits.

This banquet is for everyone, a completely inclusive event. The original banquet in the story was set for the faithful, in this case most likely for the Jewish nation, the chosen people, but many of them had bailed out. They were not going to attend the banquet. Excuses took the place of participation. Thus, the host turns to inviting others—the poor, the lame, the outcasts, the forgotten. A banquet that parallels the kingdom of God could never be just for the faithful, the "in" group, the spiritual giants. It is for everyone. No matter where people have been, no matter what they have done or not done in the past, God has invited them to the banquet.

The disciples tried to provide security for Jesus to protect him from the constant interruptions that came his way. They especially tried to screen him from the crowds, to control his appointment book, to build a wall around him. A favorite word of the disciples grew into the insistent demand, "Send them away. Send them away."

On one of Jesus' journeys thousands of people had gathered to listen to Him. It was near nightfall. There was an evening meal to worry about; the sun was beginning to set. The disciples took Jesus aside and said to him, "Jesus, send them away. Do you see all of those people out there, thousands of them, send them away. Send them out to buy their own food, let them take care of themselves." Instead Jesus provided a banquet right there on the hillside.

This refrain continues throughout the New Testament. The little children want to come to Jesus and the word comes from the disciples, "Send them away, send them away." When the blind men along the roadside cried out to Jesus, the disciples insisted again, "Send them away." When a Pharisee came, or a woman of the street, or someone who was sick, the disciples consistently responded, "Send them away, send them away."

I am afraid that the church today has baptized that theme as our own. It seems to slip out in so many ways. "Send them away, send them away. We are so busy, send them away. We are so involved in our own schedules, agendas and rituals. We have nothing left to give to anyone else. Send them away."

Many of our mainline denominations are declining in membership. Perhaps that is because we have started sounding like the disciples. Instead of saying to everyone, "Come, the banquet is now ready, come and join the celebration," we are saying, "Send them away. Send them away. We are too tired. Our church is just for the faithful, just for people like us. Send them away. Send them away."

Jesus never used that kind of language or response. Never did he focus on sending people away. All of his life, death, resurrection and healing ministry are directed at bringing in the people, welcoming and embracing them.

Jesus says over and over, "All that the Father gives me will come to me, and whoever comes to me I will never drive away." John 6:37. If anyone is hungry, if anyone is sick, if anyone is alone, let that person come to me. The kingdom of God is like a Great Banquet. Let everyone come, especially those who are on the fringe, those who would normally not be invited. We hear a refrain at the feeding of the five thousand. "Do not send them away, rather give them something to eat."

Sixteen years ago Prince of Peace Lutheran Church was a relatively small congregation, reaching out primarily to people from its own denomination who moved into the community. We did not consciously send anyone away, but I am sure that the impact of our worship and program had that effect. We were specifically geared to reach out to people who had been here before, those who had grown up in our part of the faith, those who were a part of the "in" group. For those who were outsiders, or for those who had never heard the Gospel, we unintentionally, but quite effectively discouraged them from coming.

In the summer of 1972, a change took place. We started an outdoor worship service at prime time on Sunday morning. This kind of worship was not new to me. As a seminary student, I had spent fifteen months serving as a student chaplain in the national parks. Grand Canyon in Arizona, Shenandoah in Virginia, the Everglades in Florida and Glacier in Montana were our four different home bases for the year of ministry.

During this sojourn it became clear to me that the most beautiful sanctuary in the world is the one God created ourdoors, so why not worship in this special place when the weather allows. We had worshipped two or three times a Sunday for fifteen months in some of the most breathtaking locations in America, so it was in our blood. But what would happen when we offered such an experience in Burnsville?

Miracle of miracles, the outdoor worship service became like a banquet. Many people started coming who had never attended church before or who had taken a sabbatical from worship for many years. It was not long before we had more people coming to church in the summer than we had in the winter, an almost unheard of phenomenon in this northern part of the courntry. In addition, we discovered that outdoor worship would not lend itself to the kind of worship we had indoors. Liturgy, pipe organs, choir leadership were just not possible, so at that point we discovered a more informal, contemporary style of worship. It was like a banquet. When our faithful would not come inside in the summer in any great numbers, we designed a celebration outdoors, and all sorts of strangers wandered in.

Our basic discovery was that people have very different preferences, including widely varied expectations, needs and attitudes. This insight has led us to today, and we now have three different worship alternatives each Sunday, from traditional to very contemporary. The result of these offerings has been an explosion in membership. We have grown from about one thousand to close to six thousand. We have painted a picture of the kingdom as being open and inviting to those who have been on the outside.

The message of the banquet is that everyone is welcome, not only the familiar faces, not only the church leaders, not only the rich and famous, not only the pious and the "religious" among us, but all people, no matter where they are in their spiritual growth. We have an inclusive kingdom, we need to have an inclusive church, one that is always offering the invitation. Exclusivity is out, we are like the great banquet. The banquet is for sinners, for outcasts, for those we have traditionally sent away.

As a pastor in my first parish, I had an old gentleman as visitation pastor who ministered on a part-time basis. One Sunday he was speaking from the pulpit—he was a formidable person, a huge man, massive hands, gruff, intimidating. That Sunday in his sermon he bellowed the frightening words, "If anyone comes today to Holy Communion with mixed motives, if anyone does not have pure motives, watch out! Watch out!!!" I was so frightened I wanted to hide under my chair. What selfish motives were lurking deep within my psyche! He barricaded Holy Communion. It was just for the pure, the sinless, the "in" group. I knew that I would not qualify and wondered if the altar rail would be empty during communion that week.

So the next Sunday I tried to counter his assault, as diplomatically as was possible so as not to hurt the old man's feelings. I said that anyone who comes to Holy Communion believing his or her motives are pure, maybe had better watch out! Our capacity for self-deception is legendary. Yet the Scriptures teach us that we are always a mixture of motives, some pure, some not so pure. We are both sacred and profane.

Martin Luther suggested that we are both saint and sinner at the very same time. This is the message of Baptism. The old person needs to be drowned every day, and the new person rises.

The kingdom of God is like a banquet, where all are welcomed. Holy Communion, worship, and the fellowship of the community are meant to be radically inclusive. They are meant for all people. Any action that sends people away needs to be reexamined. We are called to be an inviting church.

Many Are Still Excluded

As we look around at our world it is clear that many are not a part of the banquet. All throughout our communities, our nations, and our world, millions either have never heard, or have heard but not accepted the invitation. At the same time, many who at one time had attended the banquet have now chosen to stay away.

Therefore, there is still an abundance of room in the banquet hall. Sometimes in churches which have space problems, such as the one I serve, we are tempted to think that the kingdom of God is full. We are no longer under any compulsion to invite people to the banquet. The message of the parable refutes this. It says that the kingdom is never full. There is always that call to invite others to the banquet. "Go out," says the host, "into the highways and byways, into the prisons, nursing homes and the places where people are abandoned or neglected. Invite them to come." Above all, make people feel welcome at the banquet.

Some years ago our son Noel and I went skating together. Some hockey players were down at the other end of the rink as we arrived, shooting some pucks into the net. After a few minutes, some of the best players suggested that a game be organized. Captains were then chosen and the selection process began.

One of the leaders asked if I wanted to play, and, not wanting to admit that I was out of my league, I replied in the affirmative. As the selections took place, I learned again what it means to be marginal, to be "unwanted". This was rather new for me. When I was growing up I mostly remember being one of those doing the choosing, or at least one of the first chosen. No longer!

Finally, when everyone else had been selected for the two teams, one captain looked at the other and said quietly, but not too quietly, "Do you want Noel's father or should I take him?" This may duplicate the perceptions many people in our world have about the kingdom of God, feeling as if they're being chosen last or perhaps not being invited at all. So many all around us feel left out when the invitations to the banquet are given.

An elderly woman lived in a small town. Each week on the same day see went to the post office to purchase a few stamps. Year after year, the routine was the same. However, businesses do not stay the same, operations change. One year the post office modernized its service area, placing a stamp machine in the lobby to make it more convenient for the customers. The woman never used the stamp machine; she always would stand in line to purchase stamps from the clerk.

Finally, one day the man behind the counter said to her, "Mrs. Johnson, why don't you use the stamp machine in the lobby? It would save you all sorts of time."

"Because" she answered, "the machine never asks me about my arthritis or about my grandchildren."

Today there are many who never have experienced the banquet, who do not have anyone to share their hurts and joys, who have never heard the invitation. Jesus sets forth for us in this story the meaning of the kingdom. It is inclusive. There is still a great deal of room, and we are the ones to find someone to help fill that banquet hall.

Is your church like the great banquet? Is there a magnificent celebration going on? Are people out inviting others to come? Is there a sense of urgency about this endeavor? Remember, the church should be the beginning of Christ's kingdom here on earth. The kingdom of heaven is like a great banquet!

Chapter Six

LET ME TELL YOU A STORY

HOW TO RESPOND TO FEAR

First impressions are often crucial. The word from people who are supposed to know about such things is that you have only one opportunity to make a first impression. The Dale Carnegie course, among others, focuses intentionally on the importance of that first encounter. We are told that when we meet someone for the first time we must make sure to communicate the kind of person we want others to see. The most self-defeating result is a first impression which creates just the opposite image from that which is desired.

There is a whole-self study taking place today about the first impression made by churches. The rationale for this look inward has to do with the current resurgence of evangelism and church growth. In other words, if a church is going to reach new people it needs to be concerned about the way it's viewed by the first-time visitor. Thus, congregations are looking at all of the dynamics that go into such an impression—church signs, parking lots, entrances, friendly ushers, greeters, the quality of music and preaching—the list is almost endless. The concern is legitimate, because if a person does not have a good first impression of a congregation, chances are rather strong that there will not be a repeat visit.

Through the years, I have filed away some conclusions regarding the new visitor. People who "come on strong" during our first meeting create all sorts of warning alarms in my system. Time and again I have encountered people who have come to me as an absolute stranger, acting instead as a long-lost friend. Some of these newcomers lavish praise on you for real or imagined successes without knowing very much at all about you.

For instance, I have seen a number of people visit our congregation on a Sunday morning and then wax eloquently about the quality and inspiration of the worship service. Within one hour they are conviced that this is the epitomy of what the church should be. However, I have discovered many times over, sometimes with some pain and disappointment, that these kind of people rarely last. Often they come in with a bang and leave with a whimper.

For this reason I seem to be more comfortable with the person who first arrives with more hesitation and reservation. A person who comes on like gangbusters always makes me wonder where they will be when the first blush is over. Rome or the church was not built in a day, neither are friendships or relationships constructed at the first meeting. As some irreverent commentator has written, "It was love at first sight, but then he (she) took another look."

I wonder if Jesus was not facing the same kind of situation in the 21st chapter of Matthew. At first many people no doubt followed Jesus with enthusiastic gusto and a sense of euphoria. This was the real thing. To jump on the bandwagon would have been very tempting, but many who had been there at first soon began to drift away. Many reasons were given. The demands were too great, the hassles too common, the fear too pervasive. Many listeners must have backed away at the very time they should have been moving closer. Such fickleness must have been discouraging for Jesus.

Jesus speaks to this concern. He says to the disciples, "Let me tell you a story."

Matthew 21:28-31:

"What do you think? There was a man who had two sons. He went to the first and said, 'Son, go and work today in the vineyard.' 'I will not,' he answered, but later changed his mind and went.

Then the father went to the other son and said the same thing. He answered, 'I will, sir,' but he did not go. Which of the two did what his father wanted?"

Many different reference points could frame this chapter. Let me suggest one possible scenario, although it is by no means the only one that could be suggested. However, this line of thinking gives us an opportunity to confront one of the most significant issues of our time.

Suppose that these two sons are acting not out of freedom of choice, not out of their own initiative, but rather are responding from the dynamic of fear. Let's suppose for a moment that both of these sons have acted because of a fear of consequences. Central to this is that they are afraid of their father. They really do not want to obey him, but there is this lingering fear that will not run away.

The first son declared at the initial meeting that he would not go out into the vineyard to work. But as time passed, he may have begun to worry about some of the consequences that could come his way if he continued on this course. He certainly would not have been the first son or daughter who turned around and changed behavior because of parental fear.

His fear was no doubt well-justified. Perhaps the father would have responded harshly, cut off his allowance, or inheritance, or both. More seriously, he could have withheld his love. To disobey one's father in those days was serious business. A compelling sense of honor and commitment to the male head of the family was present then and still is. Even today in our much more casual and permissive society, the disobeying of one's father or mother should not be taken lightly.

In the second instance, the son who said he would accept the father's request and go out into the vineyard is perhaps motivated by fear to say what his father wanted to hear. He was well aware that his father wanted him to be faithful and trustworthy, to pull his share of the load. He was afraid to say or do anything to the contrary. This is a common response in us. When we are asked at times to do something, we are afraid to say no. We are afraid of hurting feelings, afraid of not being a support for others, afraid of what might be said about us behind our back. We may not want to do it, but we fear we should.

This second son soon changes his mind. When the father is no longer standing in front of him, the fear lessens and the son makes a new decision. He probably hoped that the father would either not know about his disobedience or would simply pass over this indiscretion. That was unlikely, of course, but as time went by the son most likely convinced himself that the situation had changed. He no longer needed to honor his commitment. We human beings have developed a limitless capacity for believing what we want to believe, even if it is out of touch with reality.

Fear is as old as the existence of human beings on this earth. However, many commentators today would claim that it is increasing more rapidly now than at any time in recent history. Time and again in conversation we hear the words, "I am so much afraid, I am living every day in fear. I am just plain scared." Many of our polls confirm this dramatic increase in the feeling of fear.

For instance, more people than ever believe there will be a nuclear war in the near future. Others live in terror of the rising crime rate, often driven upward by rampant drug abuse. As a result, the home security business has become one of the most lucrative industries. We are afraid of many things—cancer, economic reversals, loss of job, family problems, crises of one sort or another. In addition, the threat of world terrorism has given us a new force of evil and fear with which to grapple.

There is some validity to our fear. Anyone who watches TV or reads the newspaper and afterwards feels safe and secure, is either an eternal optimist or is very much out of touch with the real world. An airplane blown up by terrorists, a dramatic increase in the number of young people dying of cancer, the death of so many on our nation's highways—these are compelling reasons to be afraid.

Yet we must also be aware that in the Bible fear does not have the final word. No matter what the outward circumstances might be, no matter how much we may be living under siege, fear does not win the ultimate battle. We cannot as Christians sit by and allow fear to take over. There is a power, a spirit, and a hope that is stronger than any fear. Jesus Christ can overcome fear, triumphing over all the evil forces that have caused our fear.

In Christ, we are told again and again, life is not meant to be lived behind the barbed wire, not meant to be lived in the midst of darkness. We were created instead to live our lives confidently and victoriously. Jesus said, "I came that you might have life, and have it more abundantly." John 10:10. Our hope is not in ourselves or in our own resources but rather in the person, power, and will of God. Jesus continually encourages his followers with the words, "Do not be afraid. Do not be afraid!" This is a theme that needs to be proclaimed loudly and clearly in our own day. "Do not be afraid."

Many children were crowded into a refugee camp shortly after the conclusion of World Wr II. These children were mostly orphans. Their parents had been killed or imprisoned; their situation had been desperate and frightening. Naturally they were terrified. In the camp the children were given three meals a day, decent clothes, and compassionate care.

The major problem facing the camp was that many of the children were crying and fighting nightmares, not sleeping during the night. The staff wrestled with the problem. A number of attemped solutions did not work. Finally, however, someone discovered that if they gave the children some bread right before they went to bed, not to eat, but simply to have with them during the night, sleep came far more easily.

The conclusion of the camp's leaders was that the children had been so traumatized in the recent past, so often living without food, that the security of just knowing there would be something for them in the morning was enough to help combat fear.

In a sense Jesus Christ is the bread of life. When we have that bread in our lives, fear is defeated. We welcome the rest that comes at night and know there is hope for the morning. We know we will never be abandoned, and we will never be without. Jesus gives us the confidence and the power to cast out fear.

Facing Fear

I would like to explore some responses to the reality of fear in our lives and in our world.

Fear often comes into our lives very quickly. Life may have been coasting along rather well for a long time when all of a sudden we are confronted with absolute terror. Shocked, we are not prepared for it, nor are we sure how to deal with it. Should we face it head-on, or should we turn tail and run as fast as we can in the opposite direction?

When struggling with fear we must first stand and face it. Very often those things which defeat us in the final analysis are those same fears that we failed to challenge in the very beginning. Like cancer, if we fail to deal with it up front, if we try to ignore it, hoping it will just go away, it may have the final word and very well destroy us. Family conflict follows a similar pattern. If we face it when it happens, rather than waiting until we are so far down the road there is no turning back, we have much more oportunity for eliminating fear. Financial tensions are a major cause of fear today. If we tend to sweep these concerns under the rug, to ignore their presence, most often they merely intensify.

To submerge our fears is often like trying to take a beach ball and hold it under the water. It works for a few moments but eventually it explodes out of our hands. We must absolutely face our fear at some time, and the sooner the better.

Joseph Conrad in his novel *Typhoon* tells a dramatic story about responding to fear. He writes about a violent storm taking place in the China Sea. A great sailing vessel's life is suddenly in jeopardy. In the narrative a young man named Duke is asked to take the wheel of the vessel and is given the following counsel by the captain:

> "Keep her facing it. Don't be put off by anything. Keep her facing it. They may say what they like, but the heaviest seas run with the wind. Facing it, always facing. That's the way to get through. You are a young sailor, so face it. That's enough for any man. Keep a cool head and face it."

That's the best way to get through the stormy seas of life. Face them. The Scriptures counsel us time and again. In Ephesians 6:10-17, Paul encourages us to meet storms head on by being equipped. "Don't run away from the storms. Put on the whole armor of God, the breastplate of righteousness, the sword of the spirit, the helmet of salvation." In other words, put on the whole armor of God, and then stand firm. Face the storm head on.

We can race in many different directions to hide from our fears, but it is far better to face them now rather than let them fester in the future. Remember the promise that God will not give us more than we can face. We are never alone in all of this.

Are you afraid today of some problem, some situation, some person, some unknown in the future? Face those fears now, don't back down. Martin Luther responds to some of the fear that he felt in his own life by writing the words in the great hymn, "A Mighty Fortress."

"A Mighty Fortress is our God, A bulwark never failing:
Our helper he amid the flood Of mortal ills prevailing:
For still our ancient foe Doth seek to work us woe:
His craft and power are great, And, armed with cruel hate,
On earth is not his equal.

Did we in our own strength confide
Our striving would be losing:
Were not the right Man on our side,
The Man of God's own choosing.
Dost ask who that may be? Christ Jesus, it is he.
Lord Sabbaoth his name, From age to age the same,
And he must win the battle.

Action Against Fear

Once we've stood our ground and confronted fear face to face, a second step is to take some kind of decisive action. We cannot just stand riveted to the floor letting the fear overwhelm us without a struggle. We need to act. This means being intentional about our lives. We need to stand up and be counted. Fear is not inevitable; life is not hopeless. Only the cynic leaves everything passively to fate. We know there is something we can do, something we can change, to alleviate the fear.

Ellen Goodman told a sad story of a person who was so afraid of the future that he literally destroyed himself. The following paraphrases her newspaper editorial.

"He worked himself to death, which came finally and precisely at 3:00 A.M. Sunday morning. The obituary didn't say that, of course. It said he died of a coronary thrombosis—I think that was it—but every one among his friends and acquaintances knew it instantly. 'He was a perfect Type A, a workaholic, a classic,' they said to each other and shook their heads.

This man who worked himself to death was 51 years old and a vice-president. He was one of six vice-presidents, one of three who might have conceivably moved to the top spot. Jim knew that. He worked six days a week, five of them until 8:00 or 9:00 at night. To Jim it was always work. He was overweight by 20 or 25 pounds. He thought it was okay because he didn't smoke.

On Saturdays, Jim wore a sport's jacket to the office instead of a suit because it was the weekend. He is survived by his wife Helen, 48 years old, who a number of years ago gave up trying to compete with his work. A company friend said to her, 'I know how much you will miss him.'

And she answered, 'I already have.' He had three children, who, in recent years, had nothing to say to him, nor he to them. The youngest son had commented on how similar he and his father were. 'We only board here at home,' he said.

At the funeral, the company president told Jim's widow how much Jim had meant at the company and how hard he would be to replace. The widow didn't look him in the eye. She was afraid he would read her bitterness. Jim was overweight and nervous and worked too hard. If he wasn't at the office, he was worried about it.

He was a heart attack natural. You could have picked him out in a minute from a lineup. So, when he worked himself to death, no one was really surprised. By 5:00 P.M., the afternoon of the funeral, the company president had begun, discreetly of course, to make inquiries about Jim's replacement. He asked around, 'Who has been working the hardest.' "

We cannot just wait for something to happen to us. Rather, we must take some kind of positive action first. There is that old adage, three kinds of people make up this world—those who make things happen, those who watch things happen, and those who don't know what is happening. In dealing with our fears, we need to make things happen, to take some decisive action, to move off dead center. We need to get moving, to use the gifts we have been given, to walk through the open doors.

Unfortunately, fear often becomes a paralyzing force in our lives, making us incapable of positive action. It prevents us from moving on to the next step. We can become so gifted at analysis that we never get around to doing something about it, diagnosed as the age-old paralysis of analysis. The best way to deal with fear is to do something about it, something decisive. Leave the fear behind! Move to a new point in your life. Change directions!

God has something breathtaking in store for each one of us, and if we can't find it right where we are, then maybe we need to pick up our bed and walk somewhere else. Jesus' command to us in the Gospels is to "Go", get moving, do something! Don't just sit there in the rocking chair or on the recliner watching the tube. You are not meant to be a spectator in life, but a participant. If fear is dominating your life, move on.

I heard about a seriously ill man in the hospital. His family had gathered around him, wringing their hands and crying. The atmosphere was extremely depressed. But at that very moment a young, energetic Christian doctor bounded into the room, full of vitality. He was discerning as well, and it took him only a few moments to sense the darkness and pessimism smothering everyone in that room.

Looking at each person he declared emphatically, "We have to get rid of the fear germ in this room. That is the most serious illness present here, the fear germ." And in rather dramatic fashion he walked over to the window and threw it open, allowing a stiff breeze to pour into the room.

The doctor continued, "We have to drive out the fear virus from each of us, and replace it with faith." In a way, he was saying, "The Spirit blows where it wills." That was the new atmospheric condition now pervading the room.

Because fear is an attitude, one of the best tactics for combating it is to replace it with another attitude. Replace the fear with faith! Very often when I talk to a person who is afraid, who is stuck in neutral, who can't seem to break out of that cycle of despair, I discover that the person already knows what the solution needs to be. Prayers have been answered, he or she knows what ought to be done, but fear keeps them paralyzed.

Perhaps the battle against fear involves a change of life-style, of job, of habits, or of friendships. Some kind of professional help may also be necessary.

Most likely, the person already knows the solution and has been contemplating that action for some time. The problem is usually with taking the first step, moving from point A to point B. It is taking the leap of faith! To eliminate fear, we need to take some bold and decisive action, we need to stop gazing at our navel and leave the fear behind.

Remember Faith and Promise

Finally, we need to surround ourselves with the promises of Scripture and the overwhelming strength emanating from the Christian community. We seldom can eliminate fear all by ourselves. We need to find the strength that God offers to us, both through His Word and also through His people. To conquer fear, we need to be a part of a caring, affirming, scripturally-based, faith-filled community.

I believe Alcoholics Anonymous is such a healing force because it begins with the confession, "I am powerless over chemicals," and then ends with the amazing support of the caring community. When we are out of control in any area of life, when fear immobilizes us, we need to turn our lives over to the power and direction of Jesus Christ.

In Christ we find not fear, but faith; not anxiety, but peace; not gloom and doom, but joy. The gift of faith is having the window thrown wide open allowing the fresh breeze of the Spirit to renew us, just as the summer wind of a Minnesota lake refreshes us. Perfect love casts out fear.

Recently I was working out in the yard when two well-dressed gentlemen came along. They did not identify themselves but gave me a pamphlet with the words, "Do you know that the end of the world is near?" As I looked through the brochure, it was clear to me that they were trying to literally scare the hell out of me!

According to the pamphlet, the Bible says that the world is going to end in this generation, and if I was not right with God on that soon-to-be-arriving day, then I would be left when he returns. More than this, however, I also discovered that unless I was a member of the Jehovah's Witnesses, I could not avoid the holocaust that was coming my way. Only those chosen few were going to make it into the heavenly kingdom.

I challenged these two gentlemen by telling them I was not really concerned about the actual time the world would come to an end. I did not think the Bible had given us this information in the first place. Rather, it makes some strong statements to the contrary, saying that we do not know the day nor the hour. I told them that, even more importantly, I do not believe we should live in fear and trembling about the end of the world, but rather live in faith and assurance.

If the world would end tomorrow, so be it! We should be ready whenever our Lord would return. If our civilization lasts another generation, well, that's okay too. We never plant our feet too firmly on this planet anyway. We are only to be here for a very short time, almost the blinking of an eye in terms of eternity. For that reason, we live not in fear, but in faith under the Lordship of Jesus Christ. These visitors were trying to force on me a theology of fear. On the contrary, I believe that Scripture gives us a Gospel of hope.

The Christian community has amazing strength and power! It is the people who understand fear and place it into God's hands. Whenever I am most afraid I find tremendous hope and receive comfort from some of those around me who have a faith that soars to the mountains. They remind me of Christ's constant presence. When they are hurt, or confused, or weak, they find the same kind of strength from Christ through me. When we share our burdens with one another, they seem only half as heavy. When we share with two others, then they're lighter still. We know where to turn.

Often times the comic strip, Peanuts, has more theology than many lengthy and complicated books of doctrine. One day Lucy walked up to Linus. "Linus," she asked, "what is the meaning of life? What is it all about?" There is complete silence. "Linus," she asks again, "what is the meaning of life?" Finally, after more awkward silence, Linus holds up his blanket as if to say, "Meaning in life is found in my blanket. It is found in the tangible, in possessions, in things." And Lucy replies to this bit of the American way of life with her standard, "Good grief!"

Next Lucy goes to Charlie Brown and asks him the same question. "What is the meaning of life, Charlie Brown?" Charlie has his moralisms ready. "Be kind, be prompt, don't smoke, smile a lot, think happy, eat sensibly, avoid cavities, mark your ballot carefully, avoid too much sun, send overseas packages early, love all creatures above and below, insure your belongings, go to the church of your choice, and keep your ball low.

Lucy replies as only she can do, in her inimitable style, "Hold still, Charlie Brown, because I am about to hit you a sharp blow on the nose."

Lucy then moves on to Schroeder, who is, of course playing the piano. "Schroeder," she asks, "what is life all about?" Schroeder throws up his hands. "Beethoven, Beethoven is what life is all about." In other words, ultimate value in life is found in music, in the arts, in culture, in entertainment. Lucy, exasperated, cries out again, "Good grief!"

Finally in desperation, Lucy turns her back on these people and their answers and looks up into the sky. She begins to talk to the stars. "You stars up there, what is it all about, what is the meaning of life?" All is silent and finally Lucy clenches her fist and shouts at the top of her lungs, "Dumb stars!"

The answer to our fear is not found in the things of this world—in music, or culture, or even in the stars—but in the love and grace and promises of God. In fact, I think it would be a good idea for us to know some of the more hope-filled passages in the Scriptures, which offer us help with our fears and frustrations. They would be ever present, even when times are tough, if we would commit them to memory. If we would learn one of the thirty following powerful passages each day for a month, we would have a steady supply of inspiration to counter all of the forces of fear in our world.

1. Romans 8:38 "For I am convinced that neither death, nor life, neither angels nor demons, neither the present nor the future, nor any powers, neither height nor depth, nor anything else in all creation, will be able to separate us from the love of God that is in Christ Jesus our Lord."

2. II Corinthians 5:17 "Therefore, if anyone is in Christ, he is a new creation, the old has gone, the new has come!"

3. Hosea 14:4-8 "The Lord says, 'I will bring my people back to me, I will love them with all my heart; no longer am I angry with them. I will be to the people of Israel like rain in a dry land. They will blossom like flowers; they will be firmly rooted like the trees of Lebanon, they will be alive with new growth, and beautiful like olive trees...I will answer their prayers and take care of them. Like an evergreen tree I will shelter them; I am the source of all their blessings.' "

4. Phillipians 4:4-7 "Rejoice in the Lord always, I will say it again, Rejoice! Let your gentleness be evident to all. The Lord is near. Do not be anxious about anything, but in everything by prayer and petition, with thanksgiving, present your requests to God. And the peace of God which transcends all understanding, will guard your hearts and your minds in Christ Jesus."

5. Psalm 23:4-6 "Even though I walk through the valley of the shadow of death, I will fear no evil, for you are with me; your rod and your staff, they comfort me. You prepare a table before me in the presence of my enemies. You annoint my head with oil; my

cup overflows. Surely goodness and love will follow me all the days of my life and I will dwell in the house of the Lord forever."

6. Revelations 21:1a & 3-4 "Then I saw a new heaven and a new earth...I heard a loud voice from the throne saying,.'Now the dwelling of God is with men, and he will live with them. They will be his people, and God himself will be with them and be their God. He will wipe away every tear from their eyes. There will be no more death or mourning or crying or pain, for the old order of things has passed away.' "

7. Deuteronomy 31:6 "Be strong and courageous. do not be afraid or terrified because of them, for the Lord goes with you; he will never leave you nor forsake you."

8. II Timothy 1:7 "For God did not give us a spirit of timidity, but a spirit of power, of love and of self-discipline."

9. Psalm 46:1-2 "God is our refuge and strength, an ever present help in trouble. Therefore we will not fear, though the earth give way and the mountains fall into the heart of the sea."

10. Ephesians 2:8 "For it is by grace you have been saved, through faith—and this is not from yourselves, it is the gift of God."

11. Psalm 27:4,5, 13-14 "One thing I ask of the Lord, this is what I seek; that I may dwell in the house of the Lord all the days of my life, to gaze upon the beauty of the Lord and to seek him in his temple. For in the day of trouble he will keep me safe in his dwelling; he will hide me in the shelter of his tabernacle and set me high upon a rock. I am still confident of this; I will see the goodness of the Lord in the land of the living. Wait for the Lord; be strong and take heart and wait for the Lord."

12. Matthew 11:28-29 "Come to me, all you who are weary and burdened, and I will give you rest. Take my yoke upon you and learn from me, for I am gentle and humble in heart, and you will find rest for your souls. For my yoke is easy and my burden is light."

13. Psalm 145:13b-19 "The Lord is faithful to all his promises and loving toward all he has made. The Lord upholds all those who fall and lifts up all who are bowed down. The eyes of all look to you, and you give them their food at the proper time. You open your hand and satisfy the desires of every living thing. The Lord is righteous in all his ways and loving toward all he has made. The Lord is near to all who call on him, to all who call on him in truth. He fulfills the desire of those who fear him; he hears their cry and saves them."

14. Matthew 9:10-13 "While Jesus was having dinner at Matthew's house, many tax collectors and "sinners" came and ate with him and his disciples. When the Pharisees saw this, they asked his disciples, 'Why does your teacher eat with tax collectors and sinners?' On hearing this, Jesus said, 'It is not the healthy who need a doctor, but the sick. But go and learn what this means: 'I desire mercy, not sacrifice. For I have not come to call the righteous but sinners."

15. Isaiah 9:6-7 "For to us a child is born, to us a son is given, and the government will be on his shoulders, and he will be called Wonderful Counselor, Mighty God, Everlasting Father, Prince of Peace. Of the increase of his government and peace there will be no end. He will reign on David's throne, and over his kingdom, establishing and upholding it with justice and righteousness from that time on and forever."

16. John 10:14-16 "I am the good shepherd, I know my sheep and my sheep know me—just as the Father knows me and I know the Father—and I lay down my life for the sheep. I have other sheep that are not of this sheep pen. I must bring them also. They too will listen to my voice, and there shall be one flock and one shepherd."

17. Psalm 51:7-13 "Cleanse me with hyssop, and I will be clean, wash me and I will be whiter than snow. Let me hear joy and gladness; let the bones you have crushed rejoice. Hide your face from my sins and blot our all my iniquity. Create in me a pure

heart, O God, and renew a steadfast spirit within me. Do not cast me from your presence or take your Holy Spirit from me. Restore to me the joy of your salvation and grant me a willing spirit, to sustain me."

18. John 14:1-3 "Do not let your hearts be troubled. Trust in God, trust also in me. In my Father's house are many rooms, if it were not so, I would have told you, I am going there to prepare a place for you. And if I go and prepare a place for you, I will come back and take you to be with me that you also may be where I am."

19. Ephesians 4:4-8 "There is one body and one Spirit—just as you were called to one hope when you were called—one Lord, one faith, one baptism, one God and Father of all, who is over all and through all and in all."

20. I John 4:16b-18a "God is love. Whoever lives in love lives in God and God in him. Love is made complete among us so that we will have confidence on the day of judgement, because in this world we are like Him. There is no fear in love. But perfect love drives out fear."

21. Hosea 11:3, 4 "I was the one who taught Israel to walk, I took people up in my arms, but they did not acknowledge that I took care of them. I drew them to me with affection and love. I picked them up and held them to my cheek, I bent down to them and fed them. How can I give you up Israel, How can I abandon you? My heart will not let me do it, my love for you is too strong.

22. I Peter 1:3 "Praise be to the God and Father of our Lord Jesus Christ! In His great mercy He has given us new birth into a living hope through the resurrection of Jesus Christ from the dead, and into an inheritance that can never perish, spoil or fade—kept in heaven for you."

23. I Peter 2:9-10 "But you are a chosen people, a royal priesthood, a holy nation, a people belonging to God that you may declare the praises of him who called you out of darkness into his wonderful light. Once you were not a people but now you are the

people of God; once you had not received mercy, but now you have received mercy."

24. Psalm 121 "I lift up my eyes to the hills—where does my help come from? My help comes from the Lord, the Maker of heaven and earth. He will not let your foot slip—he who watches over you will not slumber nor sleep. The Lord watches over you—the Lord is your shade at your right hand, the sun will not harm you by day, nor the moon by night. The Lord will keep you from all harm—he will watch over your life, the Lord will watch over your coming and going, both now and forevermore."

25. Mark 10:27 "With man this is impossible, but with God; all things are possible with God."

26. II Thessalonians 3:16 "Now may the Lord of peace Himself give you peace at all times and in every way. The Lord be with all of you."

27. II Corinthians 1:3-5 "Praise be to the God and Father of our Lord Jesus Christ, the Father of compassion and the God of all comfort, who comforts us in all our troubles, so that we can comfort those in any trouble with the comfort we ourselves have received from God. For just as the sufferings of Christ flow over into our lives, so also through Christ our comfort overflows."

28. Isaiah 40:28-31 "Do you not know? Have you not heard? The Lord is the everlasting God, the Creator of the ends of the earth. He will not grow tired or weary, and his understanding no one can fathom. He gives strength to the weary and increases the power of the weak. Even youths grow tired and weary, and young men stumble and fall; but those who hope in the Lord will renew their strength. They will soar on wings like eagles; they will run and not grow weary, they will walk and not be faint."

29. John 3:16 " For God so loved the world that he gave his only begotten son, that whosoever should believe in him should not perish but have everlasting life."

30. Ephesians 2:8 "For it is by grace you have been saved,

through faith—and this is not from yourselves, it is the gift of God."

The story in Matthew 21 never tells us how the two sons worked things out with their father, but as an answer to their fear, and also to ours, God has given magnificent resources and mighty promises. These may not always keep us completely fearless, but they may make our lives a great deal more joy-full and hope-full.

SEVENTY TIMES SEVEN IS ONLY THE BEGINNING OF FORGIVENESS

Letting go is sometimes stupendously difficult. At times from the very bottom of our hearts, from the very center of our beings, we find it almost impossible to let go. Especially hard to turn loose is the pain, the hurt, the bitterness, the sense of rejection and abandonment that we feel. How much easier it is to just hold it in, to entomb ourselves with that malignancy gnawing away inside of us, so that nothing can wrench our sickness free. Letting go is hard to do.

Letting go usually involves forgiveness. Much of our pain and hurt has come because of the actions or inaction of another person, most often someone who is very close to us. To let go means that we must forgive. We must reach down deep for some strength or power and react in a completely new manner. Forgiving another against whom we have deep resentment is sometimes more demanding and painful than continuing to hold on to all the resentment that eats away at us.

Forgiving does not always include forgetting. We will never forget some experiences, some hurts, not even after we have exhausted all attempts to let them go. God is able to both forgive and forget, but that divine loss of memory is all but impossible for us in certain instances.

A young boy developed some very bad habits. His parents were at their wits end trying to erase them. Everything they had tried seemed to have limited effectiveness. Finally, a plan was conceived. The son was told that every time he behaved in a way which was so hurtful to his parents—and ultimately toward himself as well—they were going to pound a nail in a fence post out behind the house. Standing there as a graphic reminder of the son's disobedience, the wooden post hopefully would motivate their son to change.

The experiment began. One nail after another appeared in the fence post until soon the post was filled with nails. The disgusting image was most discouraging. Nails were coming out of that post everywhere you looked. The post itself could hardly be seen. As the boy walked past the nail-studded post, he suddenly was overwhelmed by what he saw, at the ugly sight his malicious actions had caused.

The visual impact ripped through to his core. He suddenly could see some of the pain he was inflicting on those around him. In what could only be described as divine pressure, he went to his parents and sorrowfully asked for forgiveness. At last he recognized the disastrous consequences of his actions, and he wanted to wipe the slate clean, to mend the fence.

The parents then initiated a new course of action. Every time the boy demonstrated that he had overcome one of these spiteful and self-defeating actions, they would remove one of the nails from the post. Day after day progress was made, and the nails gradually disappeared. Finally the day arrived when all of the nails were gone, and the boy ran to share his great joy and exuberance with his parents.

The entire family gathered around the post to have a look. All of the nails had disappeared. It was completely empty. All vividly could see the impressive evidence of repentance and starting over. But as the family walked very close to this designated post, something was still disturbing. The post was not back to its original form. Contained within that post were ugly scars where the nails had been. Even though the nails were gone,the scars were still painfully evident.

Forgiving is difficult, forgetting sometimes impossible. Jesus has been discussing the whole area of forgiveness in the 18th chapter of Matthew, sharing both the difficulty and the necessity of such action within the body of Christ. Jesus taught his disciples that they should always err on the side of forgiveness. He encouraged them never to let the pain and bitterness that comes between people to linger, fester, and destroy relationships. For Jesus, forgiveness is as necessary as the air we breathe and the food we eat. Life without forgiveness is not life at all.

The disciple Peter wanted to clarify his own understanding of forgiveness. Added to that, Peter may have wanted Jesus to know that he was truly paying attention, that even if everyone else would fall by the wayside, he, Peter, would go the second mile. Peter may have been feeling a bit superior to the rest of the disciples, which he was accustomed to doing at times. The scene is set for these verses from Matthew 18:21: "Then Peter came to Jesus and asked, 'Lord, how many times shall I forgive my brother when he sins against me? Up to seven times?' " The Jewish rabbis had traditionally taught that the lasso of God mandated that you must forgive another person up to three times. This was the minimum required to fulfill the law.

Once was not enough, twice was better, but three times was the ultimate a person had to give. After forgiving three times, it was perfectly proper to stop right there, to draw the line, to say that no further forgiveness need be offered. End of case.

By now Peter, who is not living in a vaccum, has been deeply affected by Jesus and his message, more than even he realizes. Is there not more to all of this, he wonders, than just following the letter of the law? Should not a person, Peter asks Jesus, forgive another as many as seven times? Let's double the number three, and add one more for good measure. How about seven times! Talk about magnanimous, seven times is far beyond what anyone would have a right to expect. Peter rises to new heights of insight and generosity.

Jesus refuses to accept any kind of absolute formula for forgiveness, or anything else, for that matter. People were always trying to pin him down, to force him to define some kind of rigid, consistent, appropriate answer, solution or action. The Pharisees loved to do this, to codify teaching into some specific rules. Throughout history this has been the favorite indoor sport of countless theologians and religious leaders. The implication, of course, is that if a person follows all of the rules and the code, then entrance into the kingdom of heaven is all but assured.

Jesus always rejected this reasoning. The Holy Spirit was to be our guide, not some legalistic codes. When we are filled with the love of God, we no longer pursue the minimum forgiveness required by the law; we don't keep score, but we go far beyond what is expected or demanded. God's graciousness and forgiveness has no limits; therefore, there should be no limit to such actions on our part as well. Generosity is not launched by a code; it is activated by the unlimited grace and love of God.

In Matthew 18:22, Jesus responds to Peter in a way that must have been shocking to the audience. "Peter", he says, "you should not forgive your brother just seven times, but rather seventy times seven." Forgiveness can be an on-going process. God pours his overflowing grace into us daily. It is like a well that never runs dry. We should also be willing to forgive in an unlimited way. We may not always forget, but we are called to forgive.

In order to clarify and amplify what he meant, Jesus said once again to his disciples, "Let me tell you a story."

Matthew 18:23-34:

"Therefore, the kingdom of heaven is like a king who wanted to settle accounts with his servants. As he began the settlement, a man who owed him ten thousand talents was brought to him. Since he was not able to pay, the master ordered that he and his wife and his children and all that he had be sold to repay the debt.

The servant fell on his knees before him. 'Be patient with me,' he begged, 'and I will pay back everything.' The servant's master took pity on him, canceled the debt and let him go.

But when that servant went out, he found one of this fellow servants who owed him a hundred denarii. He grabbed him and began to choke him. 'Pay back what you owe me!' he demanded. His fellow servant fell to his knees and begged him, 'Be patient with me, and I will pay you back.'

But he refused. Instead, he went off and had the man thrown into prison until he could pay the debt. When the other servants saw what had happened, they were greatly distressed and went and told their master everything that had happened.

Then the master called the servant in. 'You wicked servant,' he said, 'I canceled all that debt of yours because you begged me to.' Shouldn't you have had mercy on your fellow servant just as I had on you? In anger his master turned him over to the jailers until he should pay back all he owed."

What a dramatic story! Jesus could have defined forgiveness, he could have painted some pleasant pictures of grace and love. Instead he tells this story of forgiveness and the failure to forgive. Of course it is overstatement to the extreme, but it effectively communicates to each of us the central issue. God has forgiven us with no strings attached, beyond measure, yet how often we are unwilling to forgive even the most petty and mundane actions in our midst.

Look at Jesus' story. A king has a servant who owes him ten thousand talents. Remember that in a previous chapter I mentioned the definition which explained that one talent was more than fifteen times the annual wages of a laborer in that period of time. If I translate that into today's monetary terms, it means that an annual salary today of aproximately $20,000, or one talent, is worth about $300,000. A man owing ten thousand talents would be in debt somewhere in the area of three trillion dollars. This is a sum more than three times the annual budget of the United States and certainly more than the gross national product of the entire world in the first century. How this servant amassed such a debt would be most interesting but not vital to the story. Jesus wants to convey that the debt was staggering.

In the parable the king forgives the debt and dismisses the obligation simply because he feels compassion and empathy for this troubled servant. God forgives, not so much because we deserve it or because we have earned it, or even because we have made amends. God forgives because that is his nature, forgiving. Forgiveness is central to his being. It reflects the cross. The Lord forgives, not because of us, but because He is Lord.

The servant's response is disappointing to say the least. Not more than five minutes after being forgiven this incredible debt, after having been given a shocking release from an insurmountable burden, we find him trying to wring out a paltry debt from another man. This debt, since it is only a few pennies, would most likely be repaid in short order.

Disregarding that fact, the forgiven servant grabs his debtor by the throat and tries to choke the very life out of this man. Clearly this is not an act of omission. So often we simply forget to forgive. This, however, is an aggressive action, a furious attack. In a sense, the released servant is now pouring hot coals on the neck of another.

"Pay what you owe," he demands. When this directive is not followed, he then has the debtor thrown into prison, where his ability to earn the money to pay the debt obviously has vanished. All of this sounds royally bizarre, both to us and obviously as the story indicated to the listeners in the first century. Who in his or her right mind could ever do such a thing? Just imagine if you were forgiven a debt somewhere around three trillion dollars, and someone owed you a few cents. Wouldn't you let that go? The story is beyond comprehension.

Jesus is saying here that this is exactly the picture of our relationship with God. We have been forgiven the ultimate debt, the debt of sin and death, yet we will often not forgive the most insignificant wrong or hurt. This story is basically directed at us. Like the prophet Nathan in his confrontation with King David in 2 Samuel 12:1-12, the words come at us, "You are the man! You are the woman!" We have been forgiven everything, sometimes we are not willing to forgive anything.

There are a number of precious gems that can be mined from this story—truths about forgiveness.

God's Overwhelming Grace

God's willingness to forgive is beyond understanding. If you or I were God, we probably wouldn't forgive like that, especially not such a large debt. Many callous and petty people, do not deserve to be forgiven. But God is filled with unlimited grace and mercy. God is always much more willing to forgive than we are to confess, to repent, and to change. God both forgives and forgets.

A Sunday School teacher asked her class of elementary school children to describe God. The children had great difficulty with the question; complete silence prevailed. The teacher finally felt the need to clarify what she meant. "God," she said, "is someone who knows everything. He knows how many hairs you have on your head. He remembers everything about your past and the present. He even knows what is going to happen to you in the future. God knows everything, and most of all, God knows you and loves you." A rather effective speech to a Sunday School class.

Mary, a little girl with blonde hair and fire in her eyes, was not satisfied with this description. She raised her hand. "I don't think that God knows everything. I don't think he remembers everything we have ever done."

There was an anxious period of silence in the class. No one knew what to say, especially the teacher. She had never been briefed on this kind of situation in any of her teacher's meetings. She decided to follow up on this statement.

"Mary, what do you mean? Don't you believe that God knows everything? Isn't that what the Bible says?" "No," said Mary, "it doesn't say that. It says that God forgets all of those sins that he has forgiven." I believe she is correct, God forgets all of those sins that he has forgiven. "As far as the east is from the west, so far has he removed our transgressions from us." Psalm 103:12. God's grace is more than sufficient for us; God is always willing to forgive.

The Cost of Forgiveness

At the same time, we must admit that forgiveness does not come easily; in fact, it is often incredibly difficult to forgive. It cost Jesus his life. Even after the parents forgave their son in an earlier story in this chapter, the scars remained.

Recently I preached a sermon on forgiveness at our church. A couple of days later a very upset young woman came to see me. She unloaded the moment she walked in the door, "You and your forgiveness talk. It is so easy to say and so hard to do. My father sexually abused me for many years when I was a child. When I told my mother about it, she would not believe me. As an adult I have gone through two marriages with men who have continued to abuse me. I hate my father because of what he did to me, and I hate my mother because she would not stop the abuse. I don't ever want to forgive them. I don't even want to see them or talk to them again."

I was more than a little taken aback. What can you say to a person who has been through this kind of living hell? Anyone who has never walked in her shoes could never know her kind of continuous pain and suffering or the shattering affects of such abuse. I told her that I heard what she was saying, and that I could understand just a little why she was so angry and filled with hatred and bitterness. I had not lived through that kind of a dehumanization, but I could understand just a small portion of why she did not want to forgive. I also mentioned that I believe in a God who would completely understand the depth of her pain and sorrow and rejection.

At the same time, I said that the person she was continuing to hurt the most was herself. She was in a sense abusing herself, much as she had been abused as a child. Anger was eating way at her system. In order for her to find some healing, she was going to have to let go of the pain and the hatred. I am sure she will never be able to forget, but maybe she can slowly begin the process of forgiving. If she is unable to do it on her own, then she needs some kind of professional help in purging her system of the poison within.

Her broken dreams will probably continue to shatter her life until she is able to find some freedom from pain. I don't know if she will ever be able to let it all go, but she is now trying to find ways to live in the present and the future, and not in the past. She is trying to forgive what is, in a sense, an unpardonable sin.

Experience does demonstrate that forgiveness is often difficult, at times even impossible. We should never minimize the struggles churning inside so many of us. Yet when Jesus talks about seventy times seven, he is also telling us that we cannot do this only on our own. We do not forgive only under our own power, just with mustering all our resources. Rather God through the Holy Spirit gives us that endless supply of power and strength to do what would be humanly impossible. Examples abound of people who have found in Jesus Christ a willingness to forgive when it makes absolutely no human sense to do so, and who have been able to forgive far beyond their own capacity to forgive. The shining example of divine forgiveness many of us immediately think of is the one of Corrie Ten Boom who, only through God's intervention, was able to forgive a guard from the Nazi concentration camp in which she and her sister had suffered.

I am reminded of a story of Louise Degrafinried, summarized from the *Christian Century.*

> It all started early Tuesday morning, February 21st, when Louise Degrafinried's husband, Nathan, got up from bed in Mason, Tennessee, to let out the cat. Cat, as they called him, stood at the edge of the porch, his hair bristled up on his arched back, and he hissed. "What do you see out there, Cat?" Nathan asked.
>
> A big man stepped from around the corner of the house, and pointed a shotgun at Nathan. "Lord, honey," Louise heard her husband shout, "open the door, he's got a gun." Before she could open the door, the man with the gun had shoved Nathan inside, pushing him and Louise against the wall.
>
> "Don't make me kill you," he shouted, thrusting the gun in their faces. The couple knew immediately that the intruder was one of the escaped inmates whom they had heard about on the radio. He was Riley Arzenaux of Memphis, who with four other inmates, had escaped from Fort Pillio State Prison.
>
> Louise Degrafinried, a 73-year-old grandmother, stood her ground. "Young man, she said, "I'm a Christian lady. I don't believe in violence. Put that gun down and you sit down. I don't allow violence here."
>
> The man released his grip on the shotgun. He looked at her for a moment. Then he laid his gun on the couch. "Lady," he said quietly, "I'm so hungry. I haven't had anything to eat for three days."
>
> "Young man, you just sit down here and I'll fix you some breakfast. Nathan," she said, "go and get this young man some dry socks." With that Louise went to work. She fixed

him bacon, eggs, white bread, toast, milk and coffee. Then she got out her best napkins, and set the kitchen table.

When they sat down, Louise took the yound man by the hand and said, "Young man, let's give thanks that you came here and that you are safe." She said a prayer and then asked if he would like to say anything to the Lord. He didn't say anything, so she said, "Just say Jesus wept." Then they all ate breakfast.

Later she was asked, "Why did you tell him to say 'Jesus wept?' " "Because," she said, "I figured he didn't have any church background, so I wanted to start him off simple, something short, you know. 'Jesus wept" is the shortest verse in the Bible."

After breakfast, they sat there and Louise began to pray. She held the young man's hand and he trembled all over. She said "Young man, I love you and God loves you. God loves us all, everyone of us, especially you. Jesus died for you because he loves you so much."

"You sound just like my grandmother," he said. "But she's dead." Nathan said he saw a tear fall down the boy's cheek. About that time they heard police cars coming down the road. "They are going to kill me when they get here," he said.

"No, young man," said Louise, "they aren't going to kill you. You have done wrong, but God loves you." Then Louise and Nathan took him by the arm, helped him up and took him out of the kitchen toward the door. "You let me do all the talking," she said to him.

The police got out of their cars. They had their guns out. She shouted to them, "You put those guns away. I don't want any violence here. Put them away. This young man wants to go back. Nathan," she said, "you bring the young man out to the car." Then they put the handcuffs on him and took him back to the prison.

Later, she was asked, "Were you frightened?" The prisoners had killed someone also. "No," she said, "Nathan was scared, but not me. I knew that God was with me, that God had sent that young man to me for a reason. I knew God would lead me in the right direction." (Nathan and Louise Degrafinried are lifelong members of Mt. Sinai Primitive Baptist Church.)

Release

We are called by the Gospel to let resentment and hatred go. We are called by Jesus Christ to give it to him and feel the peace that release brings. God has let it all go when it comes to our sins. He harbors no resentments; no hatred eats away at him. God has both forgiven and forgotten all of that garbage in our lives that we have lugged around. We will be empowered to let it all go and feel free. All we have to do is accept this priceless gift.

At the same time we accept God's forgiveness, we must look around and ask if there is a person in our lives whom we have not forgiven—maybe a parent, a spouse, an ex-spouse, a child, an employer, a former employer, a neighbor. Are we holding on tightly to some of the pain of the past? Today Jesus says in the story of forgiveness, let it go! Don't hold onto it any longer. Open those clenched hands and let go of those tightly clenched strings that bind you to your resentments and anger. Send them to God. Let it all go! Seventy times seven, let it go! If there is resentment or hatred floating around in any of us, let it go!

All the churning inside of us hurts us more than anyone else. It destroys us much more than the other person. But more importantly, it keeps us from moving on in our lives; it prevents us from taking the next steps to a new life. Physically, we know that this holding onto the hurt can cause all sorts of maladies, ulcers, heart disease, perhaps even cancer. Poison within our system can do irreparable harm.

God has let it all go, even the ten million debts we may be carrying inside of us. God's forgiveness is paid for on a cross. "Though our sins be as scarlet, they can be as white as snow." Isaiah 1:18.

Leave your sins and hurt and bitterness at the altar, and then walk away from them! Like Peter after Easter, like the thief on the cross, like the lepers and street people and prostitutes and the prodigal son, let it all go! Let the grace of God come in and let the poison be taken away. If the Son makes you free, you will be free indeed! Seventy times seven is only the beginning. This is God's intention for each of us. Release today!

THE SEED GROWING OUTSIDE THE GARDEN

People everywhere. Crowds from every side pressed in on him. Jesus could not find a moment to himself. It must have almost given him claustrophobia. The temptation to flee somewhere else would have been great. Yet Jesus saw this as a wonderful teaching moment, one of those times when people were especially hungry for his message. This was not the time to move on, but rather a time to stay and discover the truly basic issues of life. When there are people who desperately want to hear, that is an excellent time to teach.

The logistical problem of speaking to the crowd was not all that significant. Jesus merely found a boat and pushed it out a few yards from shore. There he could have some breathing space and still communicate to large groups of people. Soon some people had found seats on rocks or hard ground while others stood, the din of the jostling bodies was beginning to quiet. Now it was time to teach, and Jesus began again with the words, "Let me tell you a story."

Matthew 13:31-32:

"The kingdom of heaven is like a mustard seed, which a man took and planted in his field. Though it is the smallest of all you seeds, yet when it grows, it is the largest of garden plants

> and becomes a tree, so that the birds of the air come and perch in its branches."

A similar story appears in Matthew 17:20-21:

> "Because you have so little faith. I tell you the truth, if you have faith as small as a mustard seed, you can say to this mountain, 'Move from here to there' and it will move. Nothing will be impossible for you."

Jesus very often told stories about the activities common to all of his listeners. As usual, he was direct and practical. He connected with real life. In these examples the focus becomes planting, one of the most simple and yet universally understood activities in the world. In order to provide a description of the kingdom of heaven that could be readily grasped, Jesus paints the image of planting.

A paraphrase of these stories sounds like this:

It was planting time. Anyone who has ever planted anything in a garden or a field will understand the importance of knowing when it is time to plant. There is a right time to plant. correspondingly, there is also a wrong time to plant, and the true gardener or farmer certainly knows the difference.

My Uncle Dayle, who was a successful farmer in southeastern South Dakota, used to tell me that the most important thing about farming was timing. The crucial dimension that separates the good farmers from the rest is knowing when to plant, when to fertilize, when to harvest, and not the least of endeavors, when to sell the crop.

I remember him taking me out to a huge storage shed and showing me a couple of the massive John Deere tractors that he owned. "You see those machines," he said, "I don't really need such big tractors. Most of the year I could get along with equipment half that size. But the reason these tractors are so important is because when it is the right time to plant, then it is imperative that I move immediately. I spend from dawn to dusk in the field during that time, except Sundays. We don't work the fields on the Lord's Day. But the rest of the time we charge ahead as fast as we can go because we may not get another chance."

He went on to suggest that we who live in the city might think that all of this perspiration put into planting is obvious. When the weather is warm, you plant, and when it turns cooler, you harvest. No great mystery about that. But he said if I wanted to see how important timing is to a farmer, I should just drive up and down the roads in this area of South Dakota and look at the farms. I could very clearly tell which farmers understood timing and which did not. Sometimes, just across the road from each other, the farms looked so different, one of them lush and green, the other one spotty and full of weeds. Often the only difference was timing.

I'm certain the principle of timing applies to all farmers and gardeners. Some people plant too soon, or they plant too late. Others throw the seeds into areas where there is almost no chance for them to take root, or they do not take the necessary care of the soil from year to year. A good farmer or gardener knows when it is time to plant and then moves quickly. Timing.

In Jesus' story, the planter has exactly the right timing. This should not surprise us at all, for it is clear by the context of the story that the planter here is divine. It is God himself, and God in the story is not only aware of the right time to plant the seed but also knows where the most productive soil is.

Part of Jesus' teaching is meant to encourage each of us to learn about planting from God, to learn something about timing and the right soil when it comes to our relationship with God. We need to know what is the right time to plant the seeds of Jesus' message and love, and what is the right time to harvest, and especially to know the difference. So many people in our world have been hurt by those who have not learned this sense of timing, who blunder through all sorts of good intentions with no comprehension of planting. Just as Paul served an "internship" before he ventured out to tell others about training period before being sent out to plant. Planting does not always come naturally; it must be taught.

The parable of Jesus makes a rather surprising statement. It tells us that the seed of the mustard plant is *not* planted in the garden. After all of our concern for timing and the condition of the soil, now we find that this mustard seed is not even put in the place of highest potential for growth, the garden. Here it would be most protected from the elements, here it would be closely guarded and nourished by the owner. In short, the plant would be much more likely to survive in the garden than somewhere else. It seems so logical that because the mustard seed is a valued plant for the owner, then it should be planted in the garden, not out in the middle of a field.

But we are missing something, a vital piece of information about the mustard plant that would escape those of us who live in this part of the world.. We have no idea how large the mustard plant will become. We don't know that if you planted several of these in a garden, there would be absolutely no space left over for any other plant.

In fact, the mustard plant is the largest of all the shrubs in the Middle East. It can grow as tall as ten or twelve feet in height and sometimes even beyond that. Its branches spread just like a large tree, reaching out in all directions. Jesus even mentions that the mustard plant becomes so large that birds can come and sit in the branches and feed on the small, black seeds of the mustard pods. Birds can't normally sit in the branches of most shrubs, but the mustard plant is more than just a plant.

What is Jesus trying to communicate to the listeners, and also to us so many centuries later? Perhaps he is suggesting that it is all too tempting for most of us to spend almost all of our efforts planting the seed of fault in our own gardens, in our own spiritual backyards, in our own safe environment. Martin Mary, in commenting upon the decline of the mainline denominations in our country, suggested that most of us never invite anyone to be a part of our Christian community. We only speak to those in our own garden about spiritual matters. In fact, he notes that in a recent poll taken by the Episcopalians, they found that the average member of that denomination invites someone else into the faith once every 27 years. I'm also sure that the Episcopalians share that number with other denominations.

Jesus seems to be saying that the seed, the Gospel, is meant to be spread far beyond the confines of the garden, out into the world, out there people may have never seen that seed before. Jesus says, on numerous occasions, that planting the seed in some of the most barren and forgotten places of our world should take a strong priority in his followers' lives.

A Story of Planting

My Grandfather's name was Sven. Sven came to the United States from Norway when he was only 27 years old, just a few years after the nineteenth century became the twentieth. He was very much alone, having left father and mother and all of his younger brothers and sisters. Attending college when he first arrived, he not only received his degree but met his future bride. She was also a Norwegian immigrant by the name of Elise. They looked forward to settling down in this new land, raising a family, and becoming a part of the burgeoning young nation.

But somewhere in the midst of their education and marriage, my grandparents heard the call to missionary work overseas. That seemed so unlikely, because these two immigrants had already left a native land to come to America, and a whole new world was opening up to them. Instead of settling in, they were considering giving it all up for a ministry somewhere else. They believed very strongly that they had heard God's call, and they were ready to go wherever God wanted them to be.

Therefore, as World War I was winding to a close, newly ordained missionaries, Sven and Elise, set out as missionaries to the island of Madagascar, located off the coast of Africa. After studying the languages of French and Malagasy, they set sail. It was a harrowing trip as the ship was forced to dodge mines planted by the Germans in World War I. I remember my grandfather telling about those early days, before there were any roads, when transportation other than walking was almost non-existent, and where most of the people had never seen a white person.

He described how he took his motorcycle and went off into the bush country, bringing the name and news of Jesus Christ to people who had never heard. These places were certainly outside the garden. Even today we hear reports of churches that were planted and nutured by my grandparents, that are still active in Madagascar. All of these were born because these two individuals, as well as many others, listened to God's timing rather than their own, and boldly moved out to make disciples.

My grandfather lived to be well over ninety years of age. I remember visiting him many times in his small house in Northfield, Minnesota, and watching him continue to read his Bible each day in four languages: Norwegian, French, Malagasy, and English. In his later years he would use a huge magnifying glass to see the small print. His favorite Bible verse remained the words of the Great Commission from Matthew 28, "Go therefore and make disciples, baptizing and teaching," Just like planting a mustard seed.

Jesus' direction to his followers today is that we should be more willing to plant the seed of faith in some of those unlikely places on this earth. Perhaps we need to plant that seed in areas which the rest of the world or our country has abandoned, in those locations or communities which have been declared off-limits for so long. For what the planting of the mustard seed would accomplish is nothing short of a miracle. It could change the whole environment where it is planted. Everything could be changed—the self-image, values, purpose, the future. In any place which has been traditionally barren, where the earth has been scorched, if a whole bunch of mustard plants containing Jesus' message are suddenly springing up all over, it could change everything! A green and lush desert could suddenly provide protection in the shade. A wasteland could become a paradise of fruit and foliage.

Jesus states that we should instinctively know, just as the gardener knew so long ago, that we cannot just keep telling others in our own garden about Jesus. We cannot only "sow the seed" in the familiar confines of our own turf. It may be that our own garden, our own spiritual vineyard may already by filled to overflowing with blessings, so that we need to be searching for new places to plant the seed, to send the Gospel, where a new tree might become the beginning of new life.

The picture is rather amazing. The kingdom of God is like a mustard seed. I can think of many ways to describe a kingdom, many parallel images, but somehow a mustard seed would not be one of them. As I mentioned in an earlier chapter, God's kingdom often seems other-worldly.

Again through his stories, Jesus counters that argument, declaring that the kingdom of God is not just out there. It is not only in some other realm, but it is right here. Yes the kingdom is eternal, yet it is present now; yes, it is spiritual, yet it is physical and worldly. In fact, it is very similar to that mustard seed, that tiny seed which is planted inside each of us and which can eventually grow to become a might plant.

Baptism

The stories of the mustard seed reminds me of Baptism. As we are touched by water and his Spirit, God is taking the seed of faith, the seed of life and hope and love, and planting it deep within each of us. We are born again and will continue to be born again and again daily as the Spirit gives us life, as we respond in faith. That seed may not appear very much at its inception, especially in the life of a baby or small child, but the story tells us the seed is there. The potential is present for amazing growth.

Remember the words of the Planter during baptism, "I baptize you in the name of the Father, the Son, and the Holy Spirit. I plant the seed of faith inside you." That is what has happened to most of us at baptism, whether we remember it or not. God's seed was planted deep inside. What a magnificent gift this is! It is that amazing grace at work again.

None of us could have ever created the seed on our own, nor could we have ever planted it within. This can only be the gift of a gracious God. Can you sense the presence of that seed today. Do you acknowledge that it is deep inside you? Can you feel something of the growth and the movement of that Spirit? Believe me, the Spirit is there. God planted that seed of the kingdom in each of us.

The seed is Jesus Christ. "It is no longer I who live, "Paul said after his conversion, "but Christ who lives in me." Galatians 2:20. Everything has been changed because Christ has been planted inside of us. We are new creatures! "If anyone is in Christ, he or she is a new creation, the old has passed away, the new has come." II Corinthians 5:17. Just like a mustard seed, when Jesus Christ is planted deep inside of us, we begin to see growth. We blossom, reach out, mature and produce some wonderful fruit. In a sense we change the entire landscape of the earth around us.

A simple story about a mustard seed must have had special impact on that ragtag group of twelve disciples. It is hard to imagine how small and insignificant they must have felt much of the time, how weak and vulnerable their lives seemed to be. It must have been exciting to hear Jesus saying, "You haven't seen anything yet! This seed of the kingdom which is now so small is going to grow far beyond what any of you could ever ask or think."

This mustard seed of faith can grow not only in your own little world, not only in your own spiritual garden, but it can spread all over the world. There can be an explosion of the Gospel, a multiplication beyond what any of us could imagine. In the book of Acts, Jesus amplifies something of the dimension of this growth in the promise of Acts. 1:8: "But you shall receive power after the Holy Spirit comes upon you and you will be my witnesses...to the uttermost parts of the earth."

In other words, you haven't seen anything yet, the smallest seed will soon become a huge tree. Jesus tells the disciples that growth is coming if they stay very close to the sun. The seed always needs the sun as well as the son. Find also the living water for the growth, the water of forgiveness and ever-present nurturing which only God can give, the water which never runs out.

Then the seed will grow, and the entire world will be changed. There is also no doubt that the seed will become so powerful and pervasive that not even this earth will be able to contain that seed. Life can be changed—the seed of faith will move mountains, change other hills into plains, bring water to parched earth and provide shelter from those areas which are exposed. As Jesus says in Matthew 17, "When you have the seed, nothing is impossible!" Nothing!

A Story of Growth

There was a man by the name of Jim. The seed of faith had been planted inside of him when he was just an infant. His parents did everything they could to nourish the seed. They brought him to Church and Sunday School and all that goes with it. He was taught to give, to share, to love. Parental responsibility was taken very seriously.

Yet in spite of this diligence, this planting and nurturing of the seed, Jim did not want that seed of faith to continue to grow in him. Every time some new growth broke out inside of himself, every time he began to bear fruit, he grew restless and would cut off the branches. As he increased in age, he stifled and fought all spiritual growth. In fact he rebelled against everything which reminded him of either the seed or the planter. Sometimes it looked as if the seed might even die. Jim's life-course was set to self-destruct.

Finally, Jim physically left his home and all those who reminded him of the planter and the seed and went to live in a place that approximated a desert, where the seed had very little chance of growing. Jim was married and divorced, then married and divorced again. Eventually he was living with new partners off and on. He was living under the haze of chemicals much of the time, moving from job to job and friend to friend. Like the prodigal son, he was on the road to nowhere. He had turned his face away from the light. The future looked very bleak indeed.

Then one day, in the middle of his self-imposed desert, Jim met some people who had carefully and faithfully tended the seeds of the kingdom within themselves. They had grown and were blossoming, just like mustard plants. Being with them revitalized him. For a parched soul like Jim, these people seemed to be an oasis in the midst of his desert.

Jim was overwhelmed, for he did not believe that life could be like this. He could not even comprehend at first how happy these people seemed to be, how loving and caring they appeared. He especially saw the sharp contrast between their lives and his. At that moment, Jim decided that enough was enough, and that whatever these people had discovered, he wanted for himself. He found that what they had was the original seed of faith, and that seed was Jesus Christ.

Jim repented, which means he turned around and started traveling in a completely different direction. Suddenly the mustard seed which had been completely hidden in his life began to grow, and it multiplied like a wildflower. Jim for the first time in his memory turned his face to the sun. He had always turned away from the source of life, now he basked in the warmth. He was suddenly content to let God's Spirit with its sunshine just bathe him in a life of joy and peace and forgiveness.

It was almost like a person lost in the desert without water discovering a brand new spring of fresh-flowing life. He drank as much as he possibly could, attending worship at every opportunity, receiving the body and blood of Christ in the Sacrament, reading his Bible, praying without ceasing. And Jim finally learned how to give himself away, to love and care and reach out. Like the wayward son in the parable, Jim came to himself.

Life was suddenly fascinating, exciting beyond any measure! New life broke out all over! When the seed started sprouting in him, people who had known Jim for many years were naturally dumbfounded. These kinds of changes only happen in storybooks, not in real life. Jim declared again and again to all who would listen that his story was real. He had been trying to take the seed of the kingdom and drown it or smother it to death. Now he had begun to let the seed grow. He became like a mustard plant, bearing much fruit, giving witness to the power and love of God.

I was called to Prince of Peace congregation in 1970. At that time it was a rather small church, located in a community that was just beginning to develop. I asked the call committee what they saw the future of the congregation to be, what kind of a vision they had for the ministry and mission of the parish.

They said to me, in an impassioned tone, this church is like a mustard seed. God has planted us deep in this fertile soil, and if the seed is properly watered and nourished it can grow beyond all human expectations. In fact, they said, now that the mustard seed is planted and is beginning to grow, it probably will not be very long before it will overwhelm this site and we will need to find more room. The mustard seed becomes a very large plant and this part of the garden will not be able to contain it. How prophetic these words came to be, as we moved to a new location six years later.

In summary, the parable of the mustard seed reminds us of many nuggets of truth.

First the kingdom of God has been planted in us. Everyone who has been baptized into that kingdom has been given the seed of faith. It is not something that we have created on our own, it is not something we deserve or even expect to find. There is always that strong element of surprise when we discover this seed of faith. Above all, it is a miraculous gift from a loving and faithful God. God is the planter, putting that seed in us because He can see the tremendous potential that is present in each of us.

Each of us can become like a mustard plant. Someone has said, "Anyone can count the seeds in an apple, but only God can see the apples in a seed." God can look inside of us and see the amazing potential, the fruit that can come from our lives. God sees that this mustard seed in us can even become a mighty tree.

Do you sense the seed of faith growing in you? Is the kingdom of God like a mustard seed in you, bearing fruit, full of new life and hope? Jesus told us this story to encourage us in our journey, to demonstrate to us God's intention for our lives.

At the same time, it is also important to see in the story that seeds do not grow to maturity overnight. The mustard seed grows rather quickly, but it still is anything but an immediate event. We live today in an age of instant gratification, when we want what we want and that means now! Many people see Christian maturity and adulthood the same way. It is almost comparable to a lightbulb, one second it is dark, the next there is brilliant light. Presto!

This message is especially propagated by the television evangelists, promising that in the twinkling of an eye we can be a full-grown mustard plant. But a seed does not grow overnight; a plant takes time to blossom. Indeed, a mighty tree can take a lifetime to mature and become what it is intended to be.

Our neighbor next door has a tree in his yard which has grown to rather amazing proportions in a relatively short time. I mentioned to him recently my surprise at how rapidly the tree has grown. It now gives shade to much of his yard. His answer was surprising, yet instructive, "I am thinking of cutting it down. The tree grew so fast that I am afraid the root system isn't very deep at all. I am afaid that, with the coming of the first major storm, it might just blow down on our house."

This is what sometimes happens when a person appears to grow in their faith in the twinkling of an eye. The seed of faith is meant to grow, steadily, surely, consistently over the long haul. We continue to worship week after week, to pray, to study, to read the Bible, to share with each other, because growth takes time and the mustard seed grows deliberately. Yet we never forget the promise, that if the seed is given the proper nourishment, sunshine and living water, it will grow and become a magnificent plant or tree.

Finally in Matthew 17 Jesus adds another dimension to this picture. "If you have faith as that of a mustard seed, you can even move mountains, nothing is impossible for you." Jesus says that each of us has within us the power and a spirit to literally change the world. We so often put ourselves down. Jesus wants to lift us out of the quagmire. You are the light of the world, you are the salt of the earth, you can move mountains. Imagine what could happen if we were filled with just a little of that kind of vision and spirit!

Countless people in our world have made a dramatic difference. I talked recently with a businessman who told me that the most influential person in his life had been Mother Theresa. She had spoken some years before at a conference in his city, and when he listened to her it changed his life. Now he gives much more than ten percent of his income to others, he volunteers significant time for helping the poor, the hungry and the destitute, and he has been a major force in focusing the attention of the

Christian community on the needs of the homeless. He has even moved mountains.

A person who is filled with Jesus Christ, with the mustard seed of faith, who is growing and expanding and blossoming, can change the world. A Christian does not so much turn things upside down, as rightside up, bringing the kingdom to bear in the midst of everyday life. Just imagine what the church can do today when it is filled with mustard-seed people! Just think of what an individual such as yourself can do when the power of the Holy Spirit is unleashed! Jesus says we can even move mountains!

The kingdom of God is like a mustard seed. Let it grow!

Chapter Nine

LET ME TELL YOU A STORY

THE MAN WHO ACCUMULATED EVERYTHING BUT HAD NOTHING

We sometimes believe that the Christian faith has to do only with the spirit, the soul. We may intone the words, "I am just a stranger here, heaven is my home." Or we may assume that our response to the Gospel is primarily about the inner life.

Surprise of surprises! Jesus centers much of his teaching in the Gospels around the area of money. In fact, he taught more about money than about any other subject except the Kingdom of God. There is more comment about money than prayer, evangelism, worship, or about being born again. Amazing.

Some people have called the Christian faith a materialistic religion, with so much emphasis on money. The ultimate concern is about the spiritual, but the physical and material are given strong emphasis. Jesus saw that every area of life on this earth was under the rule of God, including money. Especially money.

The twelfth chapter of Luke describes a teaching moment between Jesus and his disciples, as the subject turns to the relationship between accumulation and giving. These exchanges came often, so it seems, for concern with the material is never very far away from any of us. Jesus is issuing a word of caution. "Watch out! Be on your guard against all kinds of greed. A person's life does not consist in the abundance of possessions." Luke 12:15

When the disciples peppered Jesus with further questions about the specific implications of his teaching, he said to them, "Let me tell you a story." He begins in Luke 12:16-21:

> "The ground of a certain rich man produced a good crop. He thought to himself, 'What shall I do? I have no place to store my crops.' Then he said,'This is what I'll do. I will tear down my barns and build bigger ones, and there I will store all my grain and my goods.' And I'll say to myself, "You have plenty of good things laid up for many years. Take life easy; eat, drink and be merry." '
>
> But God said to him, 'You fool! This very night your life will be demanded from you. Then who will get what you have prepared for yourself?' This is how it will be with anyone who stores up things for himself but is not rich toward God."

What is the meaning of life? What gives value? How important is the accumulation of material goods in the scheme of things? Here is a story that zeroes in on the very heart of the matter. In the story, Jesus sets a framework, a value system that is very hard for us to miss or ignore.

The man in the story is an entrepreneur. He has masterminded all sorts of successful ventures. He is a man who seems to have it all. Nothing is denied! Now his abundance is so overflowing, it cannot even be contained in yesterday's barns! He must have everything he ever wanted.

An article was printed some time ago about one of the newest media evangelism stars. As the article explained, her name is Terry Cole Whittaker, a former Miss California, 44 years old, divorced from her fourth husband, and now going under the title of Reverend Terry.

She was described as taking the religious scene by storm, out-polling such celebrities as Robert Schuller and Jimmy Swaggert. One newspaper characterized her as a Doris Day version of Ghandi. *Newsday* described her as the newest and hottest of the guiding lights to emerge on the guru scene. She has been seen by an estimated one million persons each week on television, in addition to the 2500 who attend her church.

"I am an evangelist," Rev. Terry proclaims, "and for me that is anyone who spreads the good news, whatever religion." She preaches, above all, the gospel of success and positive thinking. Prosperity and abundance are her recurring themes.

In a world that is filled with abundance, Reverend Terry proclaims, "The only one who denies anything to you is you. You can have exactly what you want, when you want it, all the time." Affluence is your right, says her best selling book *How to Have More in a Have not World.* Her ministry takes in between five and six million dollars a year. She personally receives $20,000 a month in salary, plus expenses. The favorite hymns at her Sunday services include "Accentuate the Positive" and "On the Sunny Side of the Street."

A postscript to the above. I just read that Reverend Terry has gone into retirement, for the time being. But even if she does not return, someone else will gladly take her place. The kind of teaching she espoused will always find an eager, hungry audience. "You can have whatever you want, whenever you want it, all the time." It is a philosophy which would have found a listening ear in the wealthy man of Jesus' story.

The focus of this parable, however, is not so much in what this man had accumulated as in what he had forgotten. The emphasis is not so much on the ability to fill bigger and bigger barns, but rather on the incompleteness of an empty life. The man had found the secret to filling his wallet and his bank account, but he was lost down the wrong street when it came to filling his spirit.

He failed to remember so much. Three specific areas are highlighted in the parable.

Life Alone

First of all, the rich fool in the story failed to remember that life was meant to be lived in relationship with others. He had not learned, or had forgotten somewhere along the way, that life meant to include others, not just himself. He thought that isolation was a goal. He was surrounded by cluttered loneliness. He so desperately needed to discover that life was much more than just accumulating, storing and feeding his own appetite and ego. He needed to know that the world was not just a place in which he could exploit, use, consume and then discard. There is so much he failed to grasp.

Jesus brings this truth to life in the story, by the way he tells it. We find that the word "I" is used six times and the word "my" occurs five times. This man is centered only in himself, his own needs and possessions. Nothing else matters. Nothing! This is selfishness with a capital "S".

He seems to echo the words of a song, "I am a rock, I am an island, and a rock feels no pain." The "me" generation we have heard so much about in recent years is not just a late 20th-century phenomenon; it is as old as history, especially as old as the story of the foolish man who built bigger and bigger barns.

Lloyd Ogilvie, the pastor of Hollywood Presbyterian Church is one of my favorite authors. In one of his most recent books, *Making Stress Work for You,* he tells the story of a married couple in his congregation who had a great deal in common with the rich fool of our story.

This couple's situation could be described as a typical suburban marriage, recognizing of course that there is no such thing as a typical anything. But these two people fit many of the stereotypes. They were comfortably situated in life, financially secure, well-respected, and seemed to have it all.

Underneath all of this decorative facade, though, were two restless and frustrated individuals, believing that life should have so much more for them than it had thus far given. The husband held a very stressful job where he felt extreme pressure and an increased sense of burnout. The wife was plagued with a series of nagging health problems which no amount of medicating could cure.

Finally, in a fit of despair this couple came to Pastor Ogilvie for help, admitting to him that they could not get better on their own. It did not take much digging to find the basic problem in their lives. The core of the frustration and dissatisfaction was that both the husband and wife had become so caught up with themselves, so overwhelmed with the issues and needs and wants in their own lives, that they were unable to give to anyone else.

They went to church on Sundays but made almost no attempt to live out their faith during the week. They had almost no understanding of what it means to share the love of Jesus Christ with anyone else. They had turned almost completely inward, giving virtually nothing away, reaching out to no one.

When Ogilvie confronted them about their isolation and selfishness, he quickly learned that was not what these good people wanted to hear. They wanted some kind of quick fix, some spiritual pill, but he told them instead that their whole lifestyle was destructive. It reeked of selfishness. They had turned in upon themselves.

A few days later the couple returned for another counseling session. They admitted to Pastor Ogilvie, "We were very upset after the last conversation, so upset that we could hardly sleep that evening. But it finally struck us that what you were saying was true, we are beginning to realize how irrelevant and uncaring our lives have become.

"We spend more money on clothes, hairdressers, golf and dinners than we have ever given to the ministry of Christ in the church or the world. Our vacations cost more than we've ever given to world hunger. We have spent almost everything we have on us. We have also realized that our friends never call us when they are in trouble. They must think we are incredibly self-centered, and they are right! We want to change; we want to learn how to give instead of just taking."

Ogilvie then suggested to them that they try a new way of living. His challenge to them contained three parts.

First, they had to make a commitment to spend fifteen minutes a day in communication with God. Five minutes could be for prayers of thanksgiving, five minutes for Bible reading, and then five minutes for prayers of intercession, prayers for others. He calls this approach to spiritual growth "Fifteen Minutes to Freedom."

Second, the couple was to commit themselves to giving ten percent of their income to the mission of Christ in the church. They were to become tithers as the Bible instructs us to be. Behaving very much like the rich fool in the parable, they had let greed replace sacrifice. Taking had crowded out giving. They now became tithers instead of tippers.

Third, they committed themselves to spending several hours a week ministering to some people of need. It is not enough in our spiritual journey to just give money, we are also called to give ourselves personally to those who are hurt or battered or abandoned in our world. As they learned to share their faith more effectively, the couple also joined a Bible study so that their growth would be disciplined.

The meaning of life, Jesus says in the story, is not found in bigger barns, in larger estates, or in a life of pleasure and ease. Rather, it is found in giving, in a commitment to something larger than ourselves. The rich fool in the story had forgotten that life was to be lived in relationship, not in isolation.

God and Money

The rich man had also forgotten about God. In building a kingdom, he had forgotten about the King. In trying to convince himself that he was a self-made man, he had ignored his Maker. This is so easy to do. When we are busy wrestling with heavy financial decisions, when we are caught up in fighting all of the monetary wars, there sometimes is not much time or energy left to think about God or to ask God what his will might be for us.

God is shoved over on a shelf, out of sight, out of mind—at least until there is some crisis that reminds us again of his presence. But this rich fool had forgotten something basic—why he had been born, what God had intended him to be. He was traveling through this life without a road map.

Martin Luther once said, "There are three conversions in the Christian faith. There is the conversion of the heart, the conversion of the mind, the conversion of the pocketbook or bankbook." Evidently, the rich fool in the story most likely had not experienced any of these conversions. Similarly, it appears as if many people in our churches have no idea that these conversions exist.

One of the most surprising and, at the same time, disturbing observations that I have made relates to people who claim one or two of these conversions but not all of them. Many folks have no trouble at all giving some kind of public profession of faith in their lives. They are more than willing to share about the conversion of the heart or the mind.

These often are people who serve on committees, who teach Sunday School, who worship regularly, who even witness to others in their everyday lives. They truly have heard Jesus' words about being born again and take them seriously.

Yet for one reason or another, they have not experienced a conversion of the pocketbook. Words about sacrificial giving seem to go in one ear and out the other. Nothing sticks. They may give a great amount of time in services, but the wallet or bankbook remains closed as tightly as it could possibly be. They think a conversion of the appointment book will suffice.

Some of the statistics about giving that come from our churches today give testimony to the pervasiveness of this situation. Two percent of family income or less is the predominant average given by people in most mainline denominations. Lutherans nationally give about 1.6% of their income to the mission of Christ. The third conversion mentioned by Luther is sadly neglected.

Maybe this is one reason why Jesus talked so much about money, about material things. For it seems indelibly clear that he wanted each of us to experience the conversion of our hearts and minds, yes, and also of our pocketbooks. He called us to a commitment of our entire lives, of everything that we have or are. To follow Jesus means to go all the way with him, committing every area of life, including our money. Four basic commitments should be central to our journey of faith.

A. *A commitment to Jesus Christ as Lord and Savior.* Sometimes it is so easy to concentrate on Jesus only as Savior, to center only on the grace of God. But Jesus is also Lord, which means our lives are to be under His direction. We live in obedience to the will and purposes of God. As Paul writes in 2 Corinthians 8, we are to give ourselves "first to the Lord". No true giving will happen until we make this commitment. When Jesus is Lord and Savior, then it makes all of our decisions about giving a great deal easier. We can become spontaneous, giving sacrificially and joyfully.

B. *A commitment to the mission and the ministry of the Church.* The rich fool believed he was to live in isolation. We who are committed to Jesus Christ as Lord and Savior know without a shadow of a doubt that we were created to be in community, to be a part of the body of Christ, the Church. Tremendous power, strength, and nurturing flow from His Church.

Jesus sent the Holy Spirit so that the church might be given power to change the world. Sometimes people who claim a conversion of heart and mind never put both feet firmly inside the church, but Jesus gave us the church, called it his body, and instructed it to be a light, to be salt, to be a healing community, to hold up the Gospel to the world. To be committed to Christ is to be committed to the church.

C. *A commitment to give 10% of our income away.* Many people today are saying that ten percent is not enough; others say it is far too much. The Bible states clearly that a tithe, ten percent, is the benchmark for giving. Ten percent should be the goal toward which we move, but not the final goal.

I believe strongly that all Christians today, unless we are in some kind of dire financial straits, should give at least 10% of our income away. This may not all be to the church, of course, but I would hope that a strong percentage of our giving would go to the ministry of Christ through the church. We may even wish to give more than the tithe, especially when we discover the tremendous joy we receive in giving, but we should give at least the tithe.

The question is always asked about whether we tithe on gross or net income. The Bible does not address this issue directly. I believe it is up to each of us to make this decision, as God leads us. Many of us in our church have made the decision to give 10% of our gross income to the mission of Christ through His Church.

We believe strongly that our church is our primary faith community, where we are given so much. We want to give as much as we possibly can to its mission. Then we are also free to give our offerings over and above that tithe to a myriad of worthwhile ministries and causes, both in the church and also in the community. United Way, world hunger, colleges and seminaries, food shelters, and clothes closets are just a few examples of places we can give our offerings. The primary focus should be to give at least 10% of our income away. It helps to change not only our priorities and values, but also our relationships.

D. *A commitment to those in need.* We cannot be satisfied with just writing a check each week or month. We must be personally committed to others. Jesus spent His life on behalf of others—outcasts, lepers, blind, lame, poor, abandoned, even thieves hanging on crosses. Our task as well is to share ourselves personally with others, to help bind up the wounds of those in need.

A woman who attended church one Sunday morning was deeply moved as she listened to a missionary from Africa talk about her work. At the close of the service the participants in the worship were given the opportunity to make financial and prayer commitments to that overseas ministry. The woman wanted very much to respond to this need, so she completed a pledge card for that purpose. She had almost no money, but she felt she must give. The pledge was made for $120 for an entire year, which for her was a very sacrificial gift, parallelling the widow's mite.

Later that afternoon the treasurer of the church was recording the pledge cards which had been given, tabulating how much had been promised to the mission work. He came across the card of the woman. Having known her for many years, he was well aware of how poor she was, and that she did not have anything left over for this kind of giving.

Acting out of pity and generosity, the treasurer decided that he would pay the pledge for this woman, so that she would not have to give when she did not have. Right on the spot, he wrote a check for $120 and marked on the pledge card, "Paid in full." He had done this good deed, and thought this would be the end of it. It certainly was a magnanimous gesture on his part.

Several weeks later the woman came into the church office to begin paying on her pledge to the mission work. When she informed the financial secretary of her intention, her financial statement was retrieved from the file. "It says on the card," said the secretary, "that your pledge is already paid."

After recovering from her amazement, she protested, "You don't seem to understand. I made a commitment of $10 a month for the missionary, and now I want to begin making payments on this pledge. I have been saving a few cents here and a few cents there, but I haven't given anything yet. Today I want to give the first $10."

Finally the financial secretary shared with the woman what had happened, how the treasurer had seen her pledge, and, knowing that she was very poor, paid it for her. At that point, the woman began to cry. The secretary asked her what was causing her sorrow. The woman replied, "The Gospel is being preached in Africa, the missionaries are hard at work in that part of the world. Jesus Christ is changing lives, the hungry are being fed, the Spirit is at work in a powerful way, and I HAVE NO PART IN IT. I have no part in it."

The rich fool had forgotten about God. Jesus declares that we cannot forget about God, or about God's mission for this world. We are called to have a part in that ministry. We are created to be in relationship with God. Life is transitory. This very night your life will be demanded from you, the rich fool was told — death is just around the corner! We best not forget!

Giving As a Way of Life

The rich man had forgotten about love, about caring, about touching, about sharing with someone else. He had missed the essence of life, a closeness with God and with one another. There is not one mention in this story of anyone else — of family, friends, neighbors, employees, no one. The man seems to be in love only with himself and with his possessions.

There is a story of a young boy who used to hang out at one of the downtown hotels in a large city. One day he happened to be there when a beautiful and expensive automobile was parked in front of the entrance to the hotel. The boy, overwhelmed by the beauty and majesty of this car, examined it many times over and walked around it so often he almost wore a path. Almost reverently, he thought that it was the most beautiful car he had ever seen.

Suddenly as he was gazing fondly at the car, the owner bounded out of the hotel and hurried toward the vehicle. The boy saw him coming and immediately began to ask him questions. "Mister" he said, "is this your car?" "Yes," answered the distinguished looking man.

"It is a beautiful car," commented the boy. "How much did it cost?" The man was a bit taken back by the audacity of the boy, but he finally told the boy more than he wanted to divulge. "I don't exactly know how much it cost," he said. "You don't know how much it cost," exclaimed the boy. "Did you steal it?" "No," said the man with a sense of laughter mixed with frustration in his voice, "I didn't steal it. My brother gave me this car!"

This news stunned the boy and he finally said, "Your brother gave you this car? Your brother gave you this car! Mister, I also have a brother. He lives nearby. He can't walk very well. Could I have a ride home in your car so I can show it to my brother?"

The man hesitated, unsure of his response to such a request. Giving strangers rides in his car was not one of this highest priorities. But he sensed the earnestness in the boy's voice, and finally he agreed. The boy jumped in and then directed the man to his home, a run down tenement building just on the edge of downtown. "Just a minute, Mister," said the boy, "I will go and get my little brother."

Soon he emerged from the dilapidated building with his brother in his arms. He was talking as fast as he could speak. "Look at this beautiful car," he kept repeating over and over again. "Look at this unbelievable car! Do you like it?"

Finally the boy turned to the owner of the car and said to him, "Thank you, Mister. Someday I hope I will be the kind of brother that you have, a brother who will give a gift like this." The man was shocked by the reply. He thought the boy might say, "Someday I hope to have a car like this." Instead the boy said, "Someday I hope I am the kind of brother who will give a gift like this."

The rich fool might have learned a great deal about life from this little boy, that giving to others is much more joyful and fulfilling than accumulating for ourselves. I hope each of us can someday be a brother or a sister like the one in this story.

A Story About Sandy

A wealth of inspiration has come to me through a young woman in our congregation by the name of Sandy Lewis. Sandy could have lived her life primarily for herself, becoming a part of the Yuppie generation so prominent in our time. Yet she has chosen to give herself in service to others, the poorest of the poor, through work with the American Refugee Committee. We got a glimpse of her sacrificial ministry from a letter she wrote to the people in our parish:

> "The American Refugee Committee has a team of 16 doctors and nurses working in a camp called Wad Sherife, near the Ethiopian border, and I am located in Khartoum, going back and forth between the camp and the capital city. It is a nine hour drive, and now with the terrorism threat, it has become more dangerous than ever.
>
> The camp has a population estimated at between 120,000 and 150,000 people. Some say it is the largest refugee camp in the world. I have never seen anything like it and I have seen many camps in Southeast Asia. The people here settled spontaneously upon the culmination of a long journey from Eritrea, a province in northern Ethiopia. Arrivals in the camp at times have reached over one thousand people per day.
>
> The land on which the refugees are staying is Sudanese farm land, so they cannot stay here permanently. The United Nations has rented the land in hopes that the situation can be resolved soon. Sudan is struggling under a drought and famine of its own, just like Ethiopia, and cannot deal with the over one million refugees that have crossed the border in recent years.

The camp is hell on earth. Miles of flat desert with stark mountains of Eritrea rising in the distance. The camp is a three-mile area filled with sand, dirt, dust and tents. There is no sanitation. Temperatures peak in the afternoon at around 120 degrees, sometimes higher in the tents. The people here are sick and hungry, rations are only some flour, oil and salt. Not enough to keep a child healthy.

Recently in the camp, we held a toy contest and promised the prize of a bicycle to the child, who on his or her own, made the best toy out of the material available. The morning of the contest we arrived at the location for the contest, not knowing really what to expect. I remember glancing at the thermometer, and the temperature was already registering 90 degrees.

I was overwhelmed to see more than 700 children present, all sitting quietly on mats, with the toy they had made proudly displayed in front of them. Our staff was to act as judges. The children sat patiently for hours as we walked up and down the rows, examining every toy; camels and other animals made from mud, some baked to a hard glaze; dolls made from sticks with scraps of cloth for a dress, the face painted on carefully; trucks made from discarded milk tins, soles of thongs cut into round tires, and bright red crosses on the side; tea sets of clay; cameras fashioned after the ones they see daily on our necks, with bits of broken glass for lenses.

Each child gazed up at us with such anticipation as we approached. It was so much more than I expected and was prepared for. It was like a trip through their homeland of Eritrea, Ethiopia, as they showed what was familiar and important to them. The judging for the semi-finalists was completed, and so we brought out the balloons that we had managed to locate in Khartoum and distributed them throughout the feeding center.

Immediate pandemonium! Many had never seen balloons before, and instantly named them "Habooba". In their language this means "to blow". Seven hundred kids yelling, "Habooba, Habooba". I will never forget leaving the camp that day. Seven hundred kids with their precious toy in one hand, a habooba in the other, running alongside our truck as we pulled out.

They followed us for a long time, racing happily, crazily and momentarily carefree in this godforsaken place. All I could think was that these were normal kids like I had been, just like the kids I see at home. But what a life they have to live. Would you please pray for these children, and for our work with them. And would you continue to give what you are able to help these people in need."

The rich fool had forgotten three things. He had forgotten to remember that life was not to be lived in isolation, but in relationship. He had forgotten about God. And he had forgotten to remember that love needs to be found at the center of life. Meaning is found in giving to others.

It is important that we remember why we have been created. We have been blessed to be a blessing. It is essential that we remember that meaning springs not from the quantity of our possessions, but from the quality of our relationships, starting first with a solid on-going relationship with Jesus. True worth is not "the person who has the most toys, wins" as the bumper sticker suggests. True worth is measured in how much we give away. Jesus' story is for us, today. Remember the rich fool.

WHAT TO DO WHEN THE TREE ISN'T BEARING ANY FRUIT

Jesus could see the possibilities. All around him were people who had almost unlimited talent—gifted people, intelligent, perceptive, dynamic. They had entered this world with such amazing blessings which continued during their lifetime. If they only would have put their minds and hearts and powers to the task, they could have been a most significant force in the world. Jesus could see in these people more potential and possibilities than they could see in themselves, and he tried to unleash some of this in each of them.

Disappointment must have been commonplace as he continued to find people who had all of this going for them, but who were not utilizing these gifts. It must have been particularly frustrating to find people who had a deep religious commitment turn inward and missed the real mission they were called to perform. Jesus could see so many of the pious who were focusing on the mundane rather than confronting the challenged and evil in the world.

The situation parallels that which challenges all of us who have children. Most parents realize the amazing potential and gifts and talents present in those whom we have brought into this world. Most of the time we can see in them resources and inherent ability which goes far beyond what we can find in ourselves. We see a whole world of opportunity for them, if they will use and develop what they have been given.

Often frustrating to parents is seeing that our children are content with the mediocre, frittering away their time and energy on the insignificant. As parents we would like to open up the whole world for our children, throw open all of the doors of opportunity and promise to them. Yet, unless these budding adults will walk through the open doors or pursue the possibilities, there is not much we can do. We may threaten, plead, attempt to coerce, or find novel ways of persuasion, but in the end it will depend on the initiative and will of our children.

Jesus verbalized this situation on a number of occasions. In the 13th chapter of Luke, he said to the crowd, "Let me tell you a story."

Luke 13:6-9:

> "A man had a fig tree, planted in his vineyard, and he went to look for fruit on it, but did not find any. So he said to the man who took care of the vineyard, 'For three years now I've been coming to look for fruit on this fig tree and haven't found any. Cut it down! Why should it use up the soil?'
>
> 'Sir,' the man replied, 'leave it alone for one more year, and I'll dig around it and fertilize it. If it bears fruit next year, fine! If not, then cut it down.' "

At first glance, this seems to be one of the stranger stories that Jesus creates. Certainly it is foreign to the personal experience of most of us. What do we know about fig trees and vinedressers, fruit from the fig tree and manure? All of us who garden or who plant shrubs or a lawn know something about manure, but the rest of the story is obscure. More importantly, we have a difficult time understanding what any of this has to do with us.

In the first century the fig tree was considered to be the most valuable product of its kind. Not only was it a magnificent provider of shade (hardly an inconsequential fact in that hot and arid climate), but it also produced abundant fruit at least twice a year and sometimes even more than that. People took extra pride in their fig trees. Vineyards filled with fig trees would have been highly prized.

Since fig trees were such costly possessions, it is reasonable to expect that the fig tree was given all of the finest care. The vinedresser would undoubtably plant it in the most fertile and productive part of the vineyard. It would recieve highest priority for pruning, watering and fertilizing. When you have a planting of such promise, you would tend to give it your maximum attention.

In this story, although the fig tree has been given all of this tender loving care, it is not bearing fruit. Potential and promise have not been translated into success. For the three years the master of the vineyard has been watching this tree, nothing! Finally, he gives the word that his patience is at an end, cut it down! It is only using valuable space and energy and resources, why bother with it anymore! Why keep a fig tree which will not produce figs?

A strange story for us. Many today would suggest that Jesus is talking here about the Jewish nation of the first century. From the very beginning of time these are the people who have been chosen to be in a special relationship with God, Beginning with Abraham, Isaac and Jacob, God had planted his Word and his power within them.

This is the people whom God had led out of bondage in Egypt into the promised land of Canaan. In addition, this was the nation which had been given the ark of the covenant, God's very presence, and to whom leaders like David and Solomon and the prophets were given. God had poured his very life into this people, had gone the second and third and tenth mile time and again to nourish, love and protect them.

An example of God's overwhelming concern and compassion for this people is found in Hosea 11:1-4:

> "The Lord says, 'When Israel was a child, I loved him and called him out of Egypt as my son. But the more I called to him, the more he turned away from me. My people sacrificed to Baal, they burned incense to idols. Yet I was the one who taught Israel to walk, I took my people up in my arms, but they did not acknowledge that I took care of them. I drew them to me with affection and love. I picked them up and held them to my cheek; I bent down to them and fed them."

All of this personal love constantly showered on people, and yet they still do not follow. What pain is evidenced in the heart of God! Also to this nation is given the most magnificent promise in all of history, "For unto us a child is born, unto us a son is given, and his name will be called Wonderful Counselor, Mighty God, Everlasting Father, Prince of Peace." Isaiah 9:6.

In spite of all this goodness and mercy, in spite of all of God's amazing grace and love for the people of Israel, Jesus says they are not bearing fruit. When the owner of the vineyard comes looking for the fruit of the vine, none can be found. The tree was as barren as if it were planted in the middle of the desert.

In exasperation, the owner of the vineyard finally says to the vinedresser, "I wonder if I should just cut it down. I wonder if it is worth spending any more money or energy. Maybe it is time to eliminate the tree and to start over, to move on to some new possibility. Maybe it is time to just let it all go."

From one view this is a somber story, it is a picture of a God who is ready to say, "Enough is enough." To any of us who wish to be faithful children of God, we don't want to hear such words. They can easily remind us of the scarcity of fruit which we are producing. It is a story which can hit close to home with some of the following implications.

God Saw That It Was Good

First, it seems very likely that Jesus is saying something very specific about our creation. Springing directly from nature, this parable has to do with the soil, the earth, the cycles of planting and harvesting. It affirms God's creation of a most majestic world, an earth of beauty and wonder and productivity. What has been planted is not to remain as is; it is meant to bear much fruit. Yet we who have been given these resources have often done terrible things to our earth. We have polluted and exploited creation. We have damaged parts of the earth so that it can no longer bear fruit.

With the potential for a nuclear disaster ever present, we are now on the edge of a precipice. With one push of the button we can destroy the whole earth, forever. Even an accident such as the one which took place in the Soviet Union in 1986 has the potential for disaster. God created the world and saw that it was very good, but we have not always treated the earth with respect and care. Like the fig tree, we have been given a lush and productive creation, filled with possibilities. Yet when the owner comes looking, no fruit may be present.

I am intrigued by a description of the earth as God created it contained in a book by Joe McGinnis entitled *Going to Extemes.* This is an account of a trip through Alaska. One passage in that book pulsates brilliant images about the magnificence and awe of God's creation.

To set the stage, the author and two other men are exploring in northern Alaska in late summer. By accident, perhaps divine accident, they discover a narrow passageway high in the rocks next to a mountain. This tunnel-like opening is impossible to see until you are right inside of it. However, these men suddenly, miraculously find themselves standing in the midst of a broad and grassy meadow, like a religious shrine not fashioned by human hands, the most "holy" place they had ever seen. One of the men wrote about his experience this way:

"My first reaction was awe. It was like entering a massive religious cathedral, empty of people. The air was heavy with silence and holiness. Before us, almost completely enclosed in light gray rock walls, was an enchanted meadow, absolutely level. A tiny lake, like a liquid mirror, was nestled in the soft tundra, reflecting the towering grandeur. A small creek meandered lazily through the meadow, passing into and then out of the still lake.

All around the meadow were spires and peaks, some of them 2,000 feet or more above where we stood. Shagri-la! The meadow was so pristine, so silent, so still! We were not sure whether we had entered a cathedral, but it felt like we had. And given the location, there was every reason to believe that we were the first human beings to see it, to set foot on the meadow grass.

We remained hushed and still. It seem almost sacrilegious to venture further, It was awe, rather than exhilaration, that we felt. Slowly, savoring each step and almost reluctant to put a foot down where, in all likelihood, no human foot had ever been before, we proceeded through the meadow to the far end. It was about a mile from one end to the other, with the meadow at no point more than a quarter mile wide.

There we sat for many minutes and stared, in silence, at this astonishing display which had seemed to give each of us a deep and sudden and private flash of insight into the very process of the creation of the earth. We had been given a gift of immeasurable value."

In this story we can sense just a small portion of the sacredness of God's creation, the holiness, the grandeur of the world as it was when God first created it. And God saw that it was good. How tragic that we have neglected our earth so badly. God's experience and feelings must be like those of the owner of the vineyard when he came to gaze upon the fig tree and enjoy its fruit, only to find that it was barren. You can imagine his anguish and disappointment.

United States

I wonder if the fig tree could not also say something directly to those of us who have been given the gift of the United States of America. I have no illusions that somehow we are God's promised land, that we are here to save the world. Much of the nationalistic fervor that springs up today, especially when mixed with a religious interpretation, often seems extremely arrogant and self-serving.

But there is a specific sense in which our country can be seen as a sequel to that of the fig tree. We have been given an unbelievable basket of fruit and talents and possibilities. We have resources that are almost without limit or measure.

Our human resources are so myriad. We are dominated in this country by so many creative, gifted, hard-working people. We have such a strong diversity and heritage from the past, we have had such excellent educational opportunities. In addition we have a strong governmental structure, which while imperfect and inefficient, has given us an extended period of stability. In essence, we are a free people, conceived in liberty and in justice and in reverance for religious values. Almost like the promised land, we have been given a land which can be described as flowing with milk and honey, or more to the point, flowing with tremendous natural and human resources.

Therefore, I wonder sometimes what the owner of the vineyard, the true owner of the land, would say when he views the fig tree. I wonder. The list of woes in our country is almost endless—crime, poverty, hunger, injustice, homelessness, pornography, drug abuse—all seem to be out of control. Imagine a country like ours, with all of the manifold resources, overwhelmed by these tragedies. Something is awry.

Above all, it seems as if so many people in our own nation, not to speak of the rest of the world, have been left out of the bounty. In spite of many people living full and abundant lives, statistics show a growing number have been abandoned and forgotten. I simply cannot understand why, in a nation as rich as ours, all of our people cannot share the blessings. Priorities are twisted.

Jesus constantly teaches us that all God's children were created to live abundant and full lives. To have a few people in the world control most of the resources is an abomination. Bearing fruit means very specifically to center our lives on compassion and service, especially toward those who seem to be living in the barren desert. Values are amiss.

During World War II, the doctors who were on the front lines reported that they had a desperately difficult job to perform. They literally had to decide at times who should live and who should die. They carried with them three colored tags. As they moved from one fallen soldier to another, they had to place on him one of these tags.

The first tag meant "hopeless". In the doctor's judgment, this man was too seriously injured, too close to death for him to attempt any kind of assistance. Complete medical facilities were too far away to justify the effort. What a terrible decision to have to make!

The second tag meant that the injured man would most likely survive even without immediate treatment. That is, the injuries were not that serious, so the soldier did not need much attention at that time.

The third tag was the one which brought an immediate response from the doctors. This tag indicated that the soldier was seriously hurt, but if he were to receive prompt treatment, there was a strong chance he would live and recover. Since there were only limited medical facilities on the front lines, assistance was only given to this group, those who might live with treatment, but would surely die without it. It was a reasonable procedure, but not perfect.

An example of how the system worked was Jim's story. Jim had been critically injured in a battle, and one leg was badly torn apart. The doctor who examined Jim determined immediately that the injuries were too grave, he was a hopeless case. So he placed on Jim the tag which indicated that nothing could be done for him. He would surely die.

Shortly after the doctor had left, a nurse in the field noticed that Jim was conscious and she began to talk with him. She discovered that she and Jim were from nearby communities back in the United States and had much in common. She saw the tag and knew what that meant, but in the midst of their converstaion, she made a radical decision.

She decided that she could not let him die. So she broke all of the rules and changed the color of Jim's tag. It was a very risky and dangerous act. There followed a two-day trip in the back of a truck and months in a hospital. Yet Jim made it through. In spite of missing one leg, he led a full and happy life when he returned home, all this because one nurse broke the rules and changed the color of his tag.

I believe this is what Jesus is saying in the parable of the fig tree. We are to be about the task of changing the color of people's tags. This is what it means to bear fruit. Just as Christ changed our tag from "hopeless" to a "child of God", from lost to found, we can help change the tags of others. When we bear fruit, we are about the task of helping those who are now living in barren and hopeless situations.

The Church

Another possible implication of this story relates to the very comfortable pews filling the Christian Church in our land. When we begin to talk about potential or possibilities, we can readily confront the church. We have been given the gospel of Jesus

Christ, we have been given the infinite gift of the Holy Spirit. In addition, we have been blessed with so many human and spiritual and financial resources. Yet we seem sometimes to be about as effective as a fig tree that has borne no fruit. For instance, there are many congregations which do not baptize or confirm one adult person in a whole year.

Many of us come from churches steeped in the Protestant Reformation. We look to Martin Luther and other reformers as our spiritual mentors, thereby giving us a tremendous theological and historical foundation for our churches. We have a center that runs deep and true. So many of the churches of the theological left and the theological right seem to run off into the woods much of the time, following rainbows and tangents, losing balance. We who have been placed somewhere in the theological center have been richly nurtured by our deep roots and instructive history. We've been given much on which to build.

Yet for all of these gifts, for all of this special heritage, we seem to be a declining force in our land. It sometimes appears as if the mainline churches do not have enough life, or get-up-and-go power or faith to influence much of anything in our world. We continue to lose members for Christ's mission. Seeming to have so little passion and fire and evidence of the Spirit, we appear more content on maintaining the status quo. Instead of running the race, we often seem to be limping along, very much like a fig tree without any fruit.

One of the beauacratic answers to this malaise has been for various churches to merge. If you have a declining denomination, then bring it together with another so that you will grow. There is nothing wrong with greater unity—perhaps it will bring about more efficiency and partnership—but it also can accelerate the decline. I wonder if the owner of the vineyard would say that merging shrinking churches is the solution.

Dietrich Bonhoeffer, a German Lutheran pastor, who was executed by Hitler after being thrown in prison during the Nazi years, preached a sermon the speaks to our own situation. It was entitled "Come O Rescuer", A part of it is quoted here.

"You know that a mine disaster is? The moment even the most courageous miner has dreaded his whole life long is here. It is no use running into walls, the silence around him remains. He knows people are crowding together on the surface, but the way out for him is blocked. He knows the people up there are working feverishly to reach the miners who are buried. Perhaps some will be rescued, but here in the last shaft?

But suddenly a noise that sounds like tappping and breaking in the rock can be heard. Unexpectedly, voices cry out, 'Where are you? Help is on the way! Then the disheartened miner picks himself up, his heart leaps. He shouts, 'Here I am, come on through and help me! I will hold on until you come. Just come soon!' A final desperate hammer blow to his ear, now the rescue is near, just one more step and he is free.

This is how it is with the coming of Christ. Look up and raise your heads, because your redemption is drawing near. Think today of prisoners, for a long time they have borne the punishment of their captivity. Now a message rings through the prison, 'In a short time you shall be free, your chains will fall,' and the chorus rings out, 'Yes, come O rescuer!'

Think of the sick person in great pain who longs for the end of the affliction and now the day comes when the doctor tells the ailing one in a reassuring and clear voice, 'Today you will be delivered.'

Think of the person with a secret, the person who lives in unforgiven sin and loses the meaning of life as well as a cheerful nature. Think of those who strive to live a Christian life and yet fail, think of people who can no longer look each other in the eye, parents and children and spouses. Think of the hopeless mess so many are in. But let us hear again, 'Look up, raise your heads, because your redemption is drawing near. You will be free.'

But the question, will the Savior get through to us? Some will be rescued, others will not. Redemption is drawing near, the only question is whether it will come to us or will we resist. Look up and raise your hearts. Look up, you whose eyes are fixed on this earth, you who are captivated by the events and changes on the surface on this earth.

Look up, you whose eyes are laden with fears, you who mourn the loss of all that the earth has snatched away. Look up, all you who cannot lift your eyes because you are so laden with guilt. Look up, your redemption is drawing near. Something infinitely greater and more powerful is taking place. Wait a short while longer, and something new will overtake you. God will come, Jesus will take possession of you and you will be redeemed.

Lift up your hearts, you army of the afflicted, the humbled, the discouraged, your defeated army with bowed hearts. The battle is not lost, the victory is yours, take courage, be strong. Do you hear the tapping and driving as the rescuer fights his way forward. Do we hear how something in us waits to burst open and become free to move toward Christ?"

Redemption. So eloquently proclaimed by Dietrich Bonhoeffer. How relevant his words were to the German Christians and to himself as their world caved in and came crashing down upon them. How relevant also to us as we seek to find hope and direction in our own troubled world.

A Story For Us

I think Jesus is directing the story of the fig tree specifically at you and me. I personally have been given such a rich heritage. Raised in a Christian home, I have attended some excellent schools and have been filled with a rich theological tradition. Now I am blessed with a wonderful wife and family. In many ways I have been nourished and fed until I am absolutely stuffed.

Yet I often feel so barren. I feel that I am not bearing any fruit for God at all. Sometimes I believe that people around me don't even know that I am a disciple of Jesus Christ. My own family and those who work most closely with me don't see much evidence of Christ living in me. This parable indeed humbles and confronts.

Yet I take great comfort in the final words of the story. The owner of the vineyard wants to cut down the fig tree, but he is persuaded to give it one more chance. Perhaps the same dynamic is true for us—we are given another chance. Each day is a new day and we given a new opportunity to start over again, to respond to this reprieve. In Christ, doors which have been hammered shut have been flung wide open.

Life may have been far less than it was meant to be for us; it may have even been bordering on the chaotic. Indeed, our tree of fruitful work for Christ may be totally empty. Yet the good news today is that God gives us new chances to start over, to get moving again. We are given some more time, a second chance. Today is a brand new day, a new chance to worship and sing and pray and study and care for others. All is not gloom and doom. A strong word of hope rings out at the end of Jesus' story for all of us to hear. The promise is given in Revelations 3:8: "See, I have placed before you an open door that no one is able to shut."

Let us call her Mary. Mary was raised in a warm and caring Christian home. She attended the finest schools and was given a rich heritage and lasting foundation. She married a fine young man with many excellent qualities, and she gave birth to two gifted children. Her church was at the center of her life. It looked to the outside world as if Mary had it all; she was richly blessed.

But ever so perceptibly, life began to sour for Mary. Routine became boredom, and life at times became almost unbearable. She wondered about her purpose in life and where she should be headed, but all was fuzzy for her. As her husband spent long hours at his job, as the children grew older and became more independent, she did not know where she fit, where she was needed anymore. She worked for awhile outside of the home, but that didn't seem to fill the void. She felt like a fig tree which was not bearing any fruit. Most everything was barren, empty and meaningless.

Suddenly, almost out of the blue, a noticeable change began occurring in Mary's life. She became involved in a group of women at her church who were wrestling with their own sense of self-worth and meaning. She began to read her Bible, to read some books with other women strugglers, and she discovered a strong supporting community.

At the same time she was invited by one of her new friends to go along on a visit to some poor and destitute women in her city. She was appalled by what she saw. This was a side of her world she had never seen before. Purpose and direction suddenly flowed back into her. She saw so much that needed to be done. All around her other human beings cried out for compassion and justice.

Mary was transformed. For the first time in her life the words in II Corinthians made sense to her, "In Christ we are new creations, the old has passed away, the new has come." She turned her life over to the power of God; she became a new person. She had been given another chance. The more she studied her Bible, the more she grew in her spirituality. The more she grew inwardly, the more she reached out to the desperate, the troubled. And the more she reached out to those in need, the more she has been motivated to grow deeper in her spiritual journey. Life is a rich unbroken circle, not a depressing dead-end street. She is now bearing so much fruit that the whole vineyard is changing—her family, her marriage, her friends, her church, her community.

What about us? Are we bearing fruit? A cautionary not in the story suggests that our time is not endless, that there are limits on how long we are given to accomplish Christ's mission. In the coming of Jesus Christ, the Rescuer, we have been given new opportunities to begin again, to start all over, to move on.

Do you wish you could bear more fruit? Be more like a fig tree? Today is the day to begin, today is the day of the Lord! The doors are wide open. God's grace is sufficient!

THE HERO AND THE VILLIAN, A CASE OF MISTAKEN IDENTITY?

Every age looks for its heros. Something inside the human psyche wants to hold up certain people on pedestals, to praise, to idolize, to follow them. For some today that would be the politicans for in many ways they have commandeered the center of the hero stage. For others it would be professional athletes who bask in the glory of recognition and adoration. Young people often direct their hero worship at rock stars. Heroes, and/or as Manya Angelou states it "sheroes" are part and parcel of American life.

The religious community is no different. We also seek our idols, those who can be held up as models of virtue or piety or spirituality or social concern. Some denominations tend to disparage heroes, putting more emphasis on the office than on the individual. But many religious groups today unabashedly promote the canonization of heroes. A good test is found in how much of an audience certain religious heroes will attract when they breeze into town.

E. Brooks Holifield wrote an incisive piece some years ago entitled "The Hero and Minister in American Culture." He applies his principle primarily to pastors, but it could have broader implications as well. Holifield claims that heroes in religious life usually are those who conform most closely to the heroes of secular life in any particular time period. In other words, whatever is truly "in" as far as the society as a whole is concerned is what people will want to find in their religious leaders as well.

For instance, during the mid-nineteenth century, the hero of secular culture was the gentleman, the learned and refined scholar. Many religious people of that day thus became disenchanted with the rough and tumble preachers of the frontier and began to expect gentility and culture from their leaders. History demonstrates that many pastors from aristocratic ancestry arrived in America to meet this perceived need.

After the Civil War, the images from the secular magazines began to change the definition of the hero. It was now the industrial era, and the new hero of society was the man of power. Desired traits were now forcefulness, fame, far-reaching vision, the capacity to hold sway over others, and the ability to control and command masses of people. We think immediately in the secular realm of Carnegie, Vanderbilt, and Rockefeller as the heroes of that day. Religious leaders were expected to emulate these men.

By the end of the century, revelations of corruption and monopoly transformed the image of the industrial baron to that of the robber baron. The image of the hero changed abruptly. Now the hero became the progressive, the man or woman of social consciousness, one of high ideals and moral purpose. Washington Gladden, the father of the social gospel, became the leading religious hero. With a fervor for social justice, he served on the Columbus City Council and fought the streetcar company and electric light monopoly.

After World War I, the reform movement took a back seat to a new emphasis. The popular hero now became one who could mobilize the nation, the manager of large organizations. Key words were "organization" and "efficiency". The hero in the religious community now became the administrative manager, the consummate bureaucrat.

Holifield does not carry his analysis into our modern day period. But it seems clear that our heroes/sheroes today are those who have gained recognition and power via the media. In secular society the heroes are those who have dominated the television and motion picture industry. One of them is even President of the United States. Similarly, the heroes of the religious community today often are those who have become media personalities. Pat Robertson, Oral Roberts, Robert Schuller, Jimmy Swaggert, Amy Grant, and Jerry Falwell come to mind as heroes of a strong segment of the American religious community. Granted, many Christians are appalled by the adoration given to heroes, but this dislike does not have much impact on such a phenomenon.

The disciples in some sense were wrestling with the same issue. Who truly lives a spiritual life. Who in the religious community should be emulated? It was perfectly clear in that society that the most honored and most respected religious people were the Pharisees. These good folks amplified many of the themes which the culture in that day held in high esteem; impeccable morality, unwavering devotion to duty, and a commitment to generous giving.

The disciples were probing this whole arena of heroes with Jesus, trying to define the nature of the religious life. Time and again the question must have been asked, "Jesus, should we live like the Pharisees? Is this what spirituality is all about?" There is something very uncomfortable and unsettling about the piety and self-righteousness of the Pharisees, but they are such committed people! What attitudes, what basic ideals, and what kind of behavior and morality should drive the Christian?

Once again Jesus could have responded with long definitions, with hair-splitting theological concepts. Rather, he introduced his teaching with words that went something like this, "Let me tell you a story."

Luke 18:9-14:

"To some who were confident of their own righteousness and looked down on everybody else, Jesus told this parable:

Two men went up to the temple to pray, one a Pharisee and the other a tax collector. The Pharisee stood up and prayed about himself: "God, I thank you that I am not like all other men — robbers, evildoers, adulterers — or even like this tax collector. I fast twice a week and give a tenth of all I get.'

But the tax collector stood at a distance. He would not even look up to heaven, but beat his breast and said, 'God, have mercy on me, a sinner.'

I tell you that this man, rather than the other, went home justified before God. For everyone who exalts himself will be humbled, and he who humbles himself will be exalted."

No beating around the bush in this response. Jesus has the uncanny capacity to go right to the heart of the matter. We often tiptoe or tapdance around the real issues of life, majoring in minors, but Jesus seems to wade right into the debate with both feet. No more scandalous story than this could have been told. This one rated a 10 for shock value, and it left the crowd speechless.

How could Jesus have possibly said such words about the best and the brightest in that religious society? The Pharisee was the hero of the day (there were few 'sheroes" in that male dominated world), the cream of the crop. If anyone would have qualified for citizen of the year, or the good neighbor award given by some local civic group, no doubt a Pharisee would have been designated far more often than any other group. The Pharisee knew all about religious commitment, not only would he go the first and second mile, but very often the fifth and the tenth. What a hero!

The law that was sacred to the Pharisee dictated that one must fast at least once a year, which means that he would give up eating and drinking for a twenty-four-hour period. The Pharisee in Jesus' story, however, often did this twice a week. If the rule was to visit the temple once a week, this Pharisee went twice a day. Nobody did it better than this model of religiousity.

Of course the Pharisees were not naive about their standing in society; in fact, they ardently courted this kind of public adoration. Examples abound in the Scriptures about how these men wore their piety on their sleeves, holding them out for everyone to notice. As the television commercial puts it, "They gained respect the old-fashioned way, they earned it." A prayer from a first century rabbi gives some flavor of the attitude common to this group:

> "I thank thee O Lord, my God, that thou has given me a place among those who sit in the House of Study, and not among those who sit at the street corners; for I rise early, and they rise early, but I rise early to study the words of the Law, and they rise early to engage in vain things. I labor and they labor, but I labor and receive a reward, and they labor and receive no reward. I live and they live, but I live for the life of the future world, and they live for the pit of destruction."

This decided lack of humility was often most clearly displayed as the Pharisees came to the temple. The entrance was often more like a grand march, as the Pharisee would sweep into the worship place, emitting a sense of pomp and circumstance. Such a happening would almost fill the arena with an atmosphere of self-confidence and pride. They knew their way around things religious and almost everyone was in awe. Jesus, however, was not.

By way of contrast, there was the tax collector. The Biblical word for him is "publican", which means that he is even lower than the tax collector. Tax collectors, in spite of their notoriety, were basically entreprenuers. They were people who would bid to the Romans for the job of collecting taxes. Those who promised the most return would receive the position, and all monies that could be gathered over and above this bid would be profit.

Publicans, however, were the ones who did the dirty work. They were employees of the tax collectors or assistants, those out in the field. In spite of doing most of the work, they received very little of the benefits. Hatred and resentment of the publicans ran high among the people. Fraud, cheating, and coercion were all considered a natural part of this job, as it ranked right down there with the lowest of the low.

In plain language, those who were in the tax collection business were considered to be traitors by most of the Jewish population. In selling out to the Romans, they had committed a treasonous act. In essence, just as the Pharisee was at the top of the social and religious ladder, certainly the man of the year, the publican hung on at the bottom. He was an outcast, a social leper.

Knowing this, it certainly would have been reasonable to expect that Jesus would present the Pharisee as a picture of honesty and integrity, that he might hold up this man as a model of commitment and spiritual concern. In contrast to this perfect citizen, we might anticipate that he would condemn the morals and values of the publican. After all, no society could last very long if the majority of its citizens would adopt the standards of such despised and dishonest folks.

However, Jesus places a new twist into the story. He seems to smash everything that seems to make sense. As we read and ponder the words, we begin to wonder if a sense of ethics has been tossed out the window. Where are the commonly accepted standards of morality? Where is the absolute right and wrong? How in heaven's name can Jesus lambast the Pharisee and talk about unconditional forgiveness for the publican? It does not make any kind of logical sense. We are dumbfounded as he blasts the saint and blesses the parasite. Justice seems to have taken a vacation.

Yet this is a consistent theme throughout all of Jesus' ministry. He has an almost visceral spree of spiritual pride and self-righteousness. Time and again he demonstrates tolerance and forgiveness toward sinners, some of them the worst kind. He welcomes outcasts, shows love to lepers, beggars, prostitutes and tax collectors. But when it comes to those who strut around in the corridors of power, he is beside himself with anger. "Whitewashed tombs", he calls them in another passage.

I wonder if it is possible to translate this story into a more modern setting. Who would be the Pharisee, and who would be the publican? Let me climb way out on a limb. It seems possible that the Pharisee looks much like some of our leading television evangelists today, especially those who prance and parade with a sense of arrogance and self-righteousness. I am sure that we can all name certain examples without much problem.

These are the religious heroes of the day, who are featured in the leading magazines of our time, both religious and secular, and who have become self-appointed spokespersons for all of Christendom. These are the same preachers who help elect presidents, who decide what is moral and what is not. Many of these media stars have incredible power and access to power, with massive financial resources, custom-made jets to whisk them around the world. Everywhere you look the trappings of glory are blinding.

When these evangelists speak, it reminds me very much of a Bible story with a familiar ring. It seems to come out something like this, "Lord, I thank you that I am not like other men: sinners, liberals, members of non Bible believing churches, communists, infidels. I am so thankful that I am not like any of those. I am faithful to the Gospel, I have given so much to the world, I even have a corner on truth. If only our nation would follow me, then life would be on the right track. Praise be the name of the Lord, keep my name in lights, and make sure those tithes and offerings continue to flow in."

Over in the corner we have a vivid contrast. Here are all of those who are not able to even lift their heads or hands to God. Here are those in our world who have been beaten down, who are burdened by oppression and sin and guilt. The only prayer they are able to make is this, "Lord, be merciful to me, a sinner. Deliver me from oppression and fear and poverty and hopelessness. I can never be like the television hero, but please accept me and forgive me as I am."

Jesus, I believe, would still ask the same question, "Which one of these went away justified?" What do we think? I have a small suspicion that it would not be the one whose face adorns one of our national magazines and comes into our living room weekly or daily in living color.

What are some implications for us from this parable?

Pride Goes Before The Fall

Jesus articulates his abhorrence of all pride and self-righteousness, his belief that it becomes a cancer among all those who value spirituality and commitment. The danger never goes away. In fact, it becomes more pervasive as many become more deeply involved in religious life.

Some pastors and congregations in our communities consistently emit this kind of condescension and claim of absolute truth. One pastor in our community preached a sermon recently in which he said, "Everytime I take a drive through our community, I weep, because there are no Bible-believing churches here (except his own, of course)." Jesus was outraged at the kind of pride and self-gratification practiced by the Pharisees, and believe he is equally as dismayed at the exclusivistic attitude of many modern day Christians.

Richard Foster in his book, *Celebration of Discipline*, talks about the need for Christians to be centered not in domination or righteousness, but in submission. The essence of the Gospel is following the one who emptied himself, taking the form of a servant, taking the lowest place. Foster emphasizes that the most important need for each of us is to lay down what he calls the terrible burden of "always needing to get our own way." He writes about the obsession to demand that things go the way we want them to go, and says it is one of the greatest bondages in human society today.

People will spend weeks, months, even years in a perpetual stew because some little thing did not go the way they had wished. They will fuss and fume, get mad about it, perhaps even sprout an ulcer, certain that their very life hangs on the issue. So often we insist that we are fighting for some kind of a sacred principle, when in reality we cannot stand to give in simply because it would mean that we would not have things our own way.

I think this is a profound insight in a world where Christians are so tempted to believe just that. We believe that we have a corner on truth. If we are truly honest with ourselves when it comes to our own relationship with those who are closest to us—our spouse, children, parents, friends and congregation—we can see how times past which were the most difficult for us were those times when we were bound and determined to have our own way—no compromise, no giving in, a fight to the end.

This is why we have become much more comfortable with words like "self-fulfillment" and "self-actualization" than we are with words like "self-denial". But self-denial can be a breakthrough for us, when we finally realize that we do not always have to have our own way. Happiness is not only dependent on our getting just what we want, when we want it, all the time.

In many ways Jesus is declaring a revolutionary idea. In my own life I have known this truth, but I have also not known it. The greatest threat to our relationships with others is found in our desire to constantly have our own way. Most of the problems in marriage, in parenting, in relating to those around us have to do not with issues, but with a struggle for power. Who is going to win, who is going to have his or her own way?

Churches are no different. Most fights are not over theology, but rather over who has the power. Nations wrestle with the same issue. Personally, I have tried of late to give up this need or desire to always have my own way. Instead I submit, defer, and listen to the needs of others. It is not always easy, but the results are often revolutionary. Jesus' way of the cross is the ultimate example of a willingness to give up his own way, to defer, to submit. His way should become our model.

The word "sin" and the word "pride" either accidentally, or purposely, have an "i" right in the middle of the word. That is the basic problem Jesus highlights in his story and in his ministry—our attempts at self-protection, self-justification, the needs of the "i". Yet Jesus says that the only justification received by the Pharisee was that which he gave to himself. God's acceptance and forgiveness came only to the publican.

The Inclusivity of Jesus

Jesus harshly condemns arrogance among his followers. His words sound very similar to the passage in I Timothy 6:17, "Command those who are rich in this present world not to be arrogant, not to put their hope in wealth, which is so uncertain, but to put their hope in God." In other words, there is no justification whatsoever for arrogance or pride in terms of our spiritual lives. Jesus never hits anyone who is down, he never condemns the repentent. The only time he lashes out is when he sees people strutting around like bantam roosters, looking just like Pharisees who believe they have a corner on truth and a lock on righteousness.

I believe today that wherever the religious community has become self-serving and arrogant, wherever it has begun to believe its own press notices or media ratings, then the words of judgment need to be heard once again. It is so easy to trust in our own moral superiority rather than trusting in the grace and love of God. At the same time it is so tempting to pray prayers like that of the Pharisee, "Lord, I thank you that I am not like all others, sinners, heathens, unchurched. I thank you that I am not like those whose lives are falling apart. I have my life together."

I am disturbed today by the religious left and the religious right. Both, it seems to me, have become experts in the art of condescension and exclusivism. We hear people saying continually, "If you are not the kind of Christian that I am, if you don't have the same kind of religious experience that I have, if you don't believe exactly as I do on all theological and moral and political issues, then you are anti-Christian". More charges have been thrown recently between Christians of left and right and those in-between than we have been able to direct at the evil one. So much energy has been wasted that could better have been spent building bridges of understanding and reaching the unchurched.

Instead of comparing ourselves to someone else, instead of getting all caught up in self-justification, in claiming we are more spiritual or more religious than someone else, it seems we should confine a comparison of ourselves with the life of Christ. If we want to measure ourselves to another, we don't have to look around for someone who is cowering in the corner, but rather we hold ourselves up to the standards set by Jesus Christ. How do we live in relationship with Him? Are we becoming more like Jesus? Do we emit humbleness and gentleness, or do we somehow communicate envy, spite and an unforgiving spirit?

Not too long ago the phone rang early one morning in our house. It was a call from a man who was very obviously in the depths of despair. He told me that his son had just killed himself. He had taken a gun and pulled the trigger, and the police had just found the body. The family had not been active in a church. When they called the congregation where the son had gone to Sunday School, the pastor said he would be unable to use the church sanctuary because the death had been a suicide. This was a terrible blow to an already battered family, and they did not know where to turn. So they called me and asked, "Would you hold a service for our son in your church?"

Of course, by all means. We are here to proclaim the Gospel of Jesus Christ, to talk about Jesus' love for sinners and those in need. The last thing any family needs at this crisis time is to have the church inflict more pain and suffering. We certainly should not say anything at the funeral about the young man that we do not know, but we do need to see this as an opportunity to talk about the promises of God and the faithfulness of his love. A crisis can be a time in people's lives when they are most receptive to Jesus and his ever-present Spirit.

Too often churches have been like country clubs, available only for those who have paid their dues. Jesus would have said something about the Pharisee-ism in that kind of mentality, and in the story we found in Matthew, he certainly did. We are called in Jesus' name to be humble, open, and willing to serve the needs of others, not to be quick to judge, to label and turn away. The disciples kept saying, "Send them away." Jesus' refrain was instead, "Let them come to me—children, all who are weary, the lost, the fearful, the dying."

Starting Over

The center of the Gospel of Christ focuses primarily on forgiveness. As in the story of the prodigal son, the opportunity to start over again, to begin afresh always exists. No matter how much we may have strayed away, no matter how far we might have fallen, that God-given opportunity to start over again is always alive.

We are given freedom to live a brand new life. Whether it was the publican in the story or the thieves hanging on crosses alongside of our Lord, Jesus offers a new chance to start over again. For Peter who denied his Lord three times, Jesus responded with forgiveness and new life. Even for us, seventy times seven are the words of Jesus. "Jesus did not come to condemn the world, but that the world might be saved through him." John 3:17.

If the Pharisee had been a Jesus person, instead of a condemning person, perhaps he would have walked over to the publican, put his arm around him and prayed with him. When we are Easter people, then life is not found in throwing stones, but rather in showing compassion and love for those who hurt.

In an earlier chapter I talked about our ministry entitled Starting Over Single, which was the impetus for a book by that name. We have held seminars for divorced persons based on this theme twice a year for the past five seasons. They always bring us bad news and good news. The bad news is that families continue to fall apart.The good news is that many of these single people have been reached by means of this ministry. Those in attendance have found it to be healing and helpful.

As a result, our church has become known as a place for singles, a congregation which accepts those who have been battered and bruised and in many cases abandoned. We don't always do a very effective job of meeting the many needs of those hurt among us, but more and more are coming to be a part of our community.

When I was a child, I remember a large picture hanging on the wall of my room. This was the familiar painting of the Good Shepherd rescuing the one sheep which had wandered away. The sheep had strayed and had fallen over the side of a cliff and was now marooned on a dangerous precipice below. The picture, however, highlighted Jesus reaching over the side of the cliff, rescuing the sheep which was lost.

This portrays the essence of the Gospel, those who have been lost are now found, those who have been abandoned are now rescued, those like publican who have been condemned and rejected are now welcomed into the community of forgiveness.

We are not created to be either like the Pharisee or the like of the tax collector. We need to make that point clear. There is no virtue in being like either of these two individuals. Rather the message which comes through is that we are called to be like

Jesus Christ, to follow his example, to walk in his shoes, to share in his self-giving life, not counting the cost, not demanding our way. Then we will have truly entered into the spirit of this parable and discovered the power and the freedom that only comes from Christ.

THE PRICE OF BEING A GOOD NEIGHBOR

Jesus is constantly being tested. Almost continuously, he is being challenged by one group or another. So-called prophets are calling into question his credibility, scribes and Pharisees are questioning his interpretation of history, experts in the law wish to debate his understanding of the Torah. With Jesus' name becoming more and more of a household word in that part of the world, it is not surprising that he would be subject to increased testing.

In a sense, this is not all that different from our own experience. There are always people who wish to challenge our own religious understanding, our moral stance, or the measure of our commitment. Testing is not necessarily bad; it oftentimes gives us opportunities to not only verbalize our beliefs for ourselves, but to share them with others. Without testing there is a temptation to become rather apathetic and lethargic in our faith, but when we are put to the test, we often return to a sense of passion for the ultimates.

In Luke 10 Jesus is intensely tested. A prominent professor stands up in a discussion group and poses the question, "Jesus, what must I do to inherit eternal life?" No skirting the issue in this instance, no questions about whether heaven has streets of gold or silver, or if a person is married five times on this earth, which one will be the spouse in heaven. This goes right to the heart of the matter, "What must I do to inherit eternal life?" I am sure the same question has confronted each of us on numerous occasions.

Luke does not indicate in the passage how the question was asked, whether it was said with a snarl, or whether it was an honest question by one who was concerned with ultimate issues. That certainly would have a lot of bearing on how the question was received and also answered. The question could have been posed with either the arrogance which sometimes comes from the academic frame of reference, almost a desire to put this upstart in his place, or it could be the cry of a searching heart. We are not sure from what perspective the question is posed.

Jesus responds to these words with another question, a very common method of participating in a dialogue. Answer a question by asking another question. Jesus asks, "What is written in the Law? How do you read it?" In other words, "What is your interpretation of this question about salvation? What is your belief?"

The teacher replies, "Love the Lord your God with all your heart and with all your soul and with all your strength and with all your mind and love your neighbor as yourself." A magnificent answer! Obviously the man knew the law and also was able to discern the very heart of that formulation of faith. Love the Lord with all your heart and mind and strength and soul. Love your neighbor as yourself. That is the heart of the law.

Jesus commends this teacher and says, "You have answered correctly." If this had been an examination in the classroom, the man would have moved to the top of the class. But Jesus goes on to say that there is more to this than simply knowing the right answers. Orthodox beliefs are not enough. Not only knowing the information, but a commitment at the center of religious experience is required. Jesus says to the man, "Do this and you will live." Answers are not enough, action is absolutely necessary! Actions speak louder than words. Do this and you will live!

The teacher suddenly becomes very uncomfortable by this challenge to personal commitment, a reaction that may sound familiar to us. So he changes the subject. Again we are back to a kind of academic pursuit of knowledge. He asks, "Who is my neighbor?" In other words, tell me, Jesus, who I should love. It appears as if this is some form of entrapment. The teacher is trying to force Jesus to walk into a ravine with no chance for escape.

For instance, if Jesus would declare that one's neighbor is limited to the Jew, then he has placed his wider mission and ministry in a good deal of jeopardy. On the other hand, if he says that one's neighbor includes all people, all races and creeds and colors, then the Jews will probably chase him out of town. Nothing comes easily when you are being tested. Again, for Jesus the stakes are rather high.

However, Jesus answers this question as he has done so often with the words, "Let me tell you a story."
Luke 10:30-35:

> "A man was going down from Jerusalem to Jericho, when he fell into the hands of robbers. They stripped him of his clothes, beat him and went away, leaving him half dead. A priest happened to be going down the same road, and when he saw the man, he passed by on the other side.
>
> So too, a Levite, when he came to the place and saw him, passed by on the other side. But a Samaritan, as he traveled, came where the man was; and when he saw him, he took pity on him. He went to him and bandaged his wounds, pouring on oil and wine. Then he put the man on his own donkey, took him to an inn and took care of him. The next day he took out two silver coins and gave them to the innkeeper. 'Look after him,' he said, 'and when I return, I will reimburse you for any extra expense you may have.' "

Continuing with verses 36 & 37, Jesus turns the table on the teacher and asks him a question, "Which of these three do you think was a neighbor to the man who fell into the hands of robbers?" The expert in the law replied, "The one who had mercy on him." Jesus told him, "Go and do likewise."

What a brilliant story! It completely reinterpreted the teaching of the law. It broadened the concept of who was a neighbor. It centered in compassion rather than exclusion. It is so rich we could sit and mine from it all day long.

This story would have struck a responsive chord in all who listened as the path from Jerusalem to Jericho was most familiar to them all. Only 17 miles in distance, the road decreased in elevation by some 3400 feet in that short stretch. Obviously, with that kind of terrain, endless cliffs and crevices and other places for robbers to hide abounded. Probably many who listened to Jesus that day had also been attacked at one time or another.

The result of the mugging is that a man is lying battered and bleeding on the side of the road. This is not unlike the experience many of us have going through life, trying to walk a path, trying to complete a journey. We are knocked down time and again, battered and bruised by the many destructive forces along the way. Perhaps each of us know people who have been stripped and left naked or vulnerable because of the tragedy and pain and suffering that has occurred.

Think about them for a moment. Some of them may be children, women, minorities, or those who have been left out of the mainstream of life. All along the road that we travel rejected and abandoned people are strewn. The first century story is immediately applicable to every other moment in history, for people continue to suffer. Keep these people in mind as you listen to the story.

First, a priest hurries by, crossing on the other side. Next a Levite does exactly the same thing. Both of these men happen to be religious leaders, who find their livelihood and purpose in life in the all of their religious exercises. Yet they have no time for a battered man lying injured and helpless alongside the road.

Somehow religious activity for them does not cover aiding someone in need. Maybe they have an erroneous interpretation of "religious."

These two men are not unlike so many of us who are wrapped up in the life of the church. Frantic activity and business as usual can so overwhelm us and so direct our efforts inward that we are no longer even aware of the needs of the world outside our walls. Often the church can be so concerned about the survival and maintenance of the organization that it no longer is relevant to the needs of the oppressed. That can be a tragic dimension to the church, certainly not the whole picture, but real enough to give us much cause for concern.

Compassion

A Samaritan happens by, and when he sees the bleeding man lying on the roadside his heart is filled with pity. Other translations use the word "compassion", a much more fitting word today, I believe. Pity is often used condescendingly. When we pity someone, it often comes from a perspective of superiority. We intone effortlessly, "Poor man." Compassion is an action-packed word of love, of empathy, of standing alongside of, rather than looking down. The Samaritan had compassion; he stopped to help.

As this scene unfolds, we cannot help but wonder if the Samaritan had not experienced some similar tragedy in his own life. Very often people who have gone through the valley of the shadow are much more in tune with those in like situations. Those who have been knocked down and battered about are often far more sensitive to the pain of others. I wonder if this Samaritan had not seen much suffering in his own life. He stopped to help.

A young doctor was asked what had motivated him, moved him, to pursue the direction of medicine as a profession. "Well," he said, "I really had no choice. When I was only seven years old, our whole family was trapped in a blizzard for several days. During that time, my younger sister became critically ill, and the doctor had to walk four hours through the snow to be at her bedside. It was a terrifying time in our lives.

Hour after hour my parents and I sat and prayed and cried, all throughout the night. Finally, after what seemed to be an eternity, the doctor emerged from my sister's room and with bloodshot eyes and a very drawn face he took the hands of my parents and said to them, 'God has answered our prayers, he has used me as his servant, and your daughter will get well.' "

The doctor said that when he saw the faces of his parents, when he saw the expression of joy and relief, when he experienced with them the release of tears of happiness, it was at that moment he knew he had no choice. He wanted to be a doctor. He wanted to spend his entire life helping parents in similar situations to experience that kind of joy and new life.

I worry sometimes that television has blunted our sense of compassion. With so many tragedies and heartaches pumped out on the screen twenty-four hours a day, it becomes increasingly difficult to muster much passion, let alone compassion for anything. How many disasters can we take before we finally turn the bloody tube off? The results of all of this over-saturation is that we simply stop hearing the cries of the world, and that is a profound loss.

It was said of Jesus on numerouus occasions that he had compassion for people. He looked at individuals and their needs and immediately his heart was overflowing with love. Like the priest and the Levite, however, we find it far easier to ignore the suffering than to stop and stoop to alleviate it.

The Samaritan first tended to the man by pouring oil and wine on his wounds and placing bandages on them. Oil and wine were regarded in that day as effective healing agents. Today we might use other kinds of ointments and salves to prevent infection and to facilitate recovery. Finally, he lifted the man from the ground and placed him on his own animal, so he could be transported to a place of safety.

The Inn

I find it very interesting that the Samaritan took the injured man to an inn. Why not to a hospital? Why not to a doctor or a nurse? Today it is so easy to always call the professional whenever there is any kind of problem—call the physician, call the police, call the clergy, call the counselor—rather than attempting to minister as one person to another. Certainly many times we must call the expert, but so often we have the opportunity to be in the front line of compassion and healing, yet defer to someone else. We have been called to touch and soothe and nurture and help bind up the wounds of others, not just to run to the nearest phone. With government cutbacks in the works these days, we may find there is not one at the other end of the phone when we call.

The Church of Jesus Christ should be the kind of an "inn" where people will bring those in our world who are battered and hurt. Is your church or my church that kind of a place, where people might bring those they have discovered who are wounded or abandoned? Is your church or mine the kind of oasis where people will bring those who have no hope?

Is your church or mine the kind of place where we can offer spiritual help to those who have watched their marriage or family fall apart, who have lost a job or a farm, who have struggled with some kind of chemical abuse, who suffer some kind of illness or pain? Can people be brought or come on their own to our church and find a healing inn?

One of the great storytellers of our time is Garrison Keilor, the originator of the "Prarie Home Companion" program broadcast around the U.S. on public radio. He is able to articulate events and experiences which touch everyone who listens, which give shape and focus to much of life that we have either forgotten or ignored. The paraphrase of one of his monologues which follows parallels the image of the church as a healing inn.

The day finally came when he was able to enter the junior high school, which was a part of Lake Wobegon, Minnesota, High

School. Climbing on the bus for that first ride into town to school, he was now entering an entirely different world. One of the most memorable moments of that first day was the moment when the principal handed out little pieces of paper to all new incoming students, each containing the name of a family in that town.

The principal explained that this slip of paper contained the name of their "storm home." In other words, if at any time through the year a storm occurred during the school day, and it was impossible for the buses to return the students to their homes, they would then stay in town at their "storm home." I found in talking with people from smaller communities in Minnesota that this was indeed a common practice, to be assigned a storm home, a place of shelter in the event of inclement weather.

Keilor said that he was given the name of an elderly couple named the Krugers, who lived in a beautiful little green cottage down by the shores of the lake. It was such a picturesque setting, with a perfectly manicured lawn, an ornate birdbath, and two bronze deer grazing contentedly in the front yard.

He said that the little home looked so inviting, the kind of a home that if you were lost in the woods and you came upon it, you would know an older couple lived inside who were kind and caring and would take you in any time of the day or night.

He said he thought many times about stopping in to say "hello" to the Krugers. He could just imagine himself walking up to the front door, ringing the bell, and then saying as the door opened, "Hi, I'm your storm child." Then Mrs. Kruger would say as she saw who it was, "Oh, it's you!", She would call to her husband, "Come down and see who it is here. It is our storm child!"

Garrison said that he never did make it to his storm home during his school days. Blizzards always seem to arrive during the evening or on weekends; he called them "convenient blizzards." But he said he always knew that he could go there if he needed to. If his problems were ever more than he could face, he always knew that there was a home where he would be accepted and loved. It was such a comfort to him during all of those years of school to know that he had a storm home, a place to be welcomed and loved.

A storm home has a definite appeal. In the neighborhood where I live many homes have a picture of helping hands in the windows, created as safe homes for children. These remind me in a way of storm homes. Not only children need to have storm homes though, adults do too.

We too need a shelter when the blizzards are so fierce that we can't even stand up against the storm. We need a haven when the tears well up in our eyes and we can't see where we are going. Maybe each of us needs a storm home, where we can be protected from all of the elements, where we can feel safe and secure and know we are truly loved.

I believe this is what the church is meant to be. It certainly was the image that was framed from its very beginning. A storm home. Rev. Milton Cunningham, a Baptist pastor from Houston, Texas, amplified this picture as he spoke at a recent Billy Graham School of Evangelism workshop. He said, "Everyone who comes to our church has a broken heart. Everyone in our church has a broken heart." It sounds like Jesus when he said that the well have no need of a physician, but that the Gospel is meant for those who are ill.

A mother had seven sons. These sons would often tease her incessantly, "Mother," they would insist, "Which of us do you love the most? Which of your seven sons do you love more than any other?" Their mother would always answer with seriousness, "I love each one of you equally." The sons persisted, "Mother, you can't love each of us the same, which one of us do you love the most?"

Finally, the mother put it all into perspective when she replied to this teasing, "Do you want to know which of you I love the most? Well, I will tell you. I love the son most of all who needs me the most! This child I love more than any other, the one who needs me the most!"

One of the great hymns of the church says it this way:

"Children of the heavenly Father Safely in his bosom gather; Nestling bird or star in heaven Such a refuge ne'er was given.

God his own doth tend and nourish, In his holy courts they flourish. From all evil things he spares them, In his mighty arms he bears them.

Neither life nor death shall ever From the Lord his children sever; Unto them his grace he showeth, And their sorrows all he knoweth.

Though he giveth or he taketh, God his children ne'er forsaketh; His the loving purpose solely To preserve them pure and holy."

The church should be a storm home, a refuge and strength for all who are hurt and need compassion. Jesus exemplified this compassion in his life and told us to do likewise.

Dying to Oneself

Another possible interpretation regarding the bringing of the wounded man to the inn raises new awareness in this story. Dr. Kenneth Bailey, a New Testament professor who has spent most of his life in the Middle East, says that this story of the Good Samaritan might be very similar to the environment in Dodge City, Kansas, around 1850.

What would have happened if an Indian would have found a cowboy with some arrows in him lying by the roadside? What would have happened if this compassionate Native American would have put the injured man on his horse and then brought him into Dodge City? What kind of reception would have faced the Indian? Most likely it would have meant death.

Very plausibly a parallel risk confronted the Samaritan. He was traveling in hostile territory, and if he brought an injured man to a local inn, the word conceivably would have spread like wildfire, and this man's life might have been in danger. Dr. Bailey says that in that part of the world people often first act angrily and violently, and then ask questions later. The villagers would have more than likely have believed that the Samaritan had something to do with the condition of the injured man. Samaritans were despised creatures. Any pretext for doing away with one of them would have been seized.

Thus, this parable can be a foretaste, a picture of what will happen to Jesus himself. Like the Good Samaritan, Jesus will pay for the outpouring of his compassion and love with his life. The parable, therefore, can be another New Testament prediction of the death that Jesus is to die.

The final part of this story concerns the payment of money by the Samaritan on behalf of the victim. He takes out two silver coins and gives them to the innkeeper. "Take care of him," he says, "and when I come back this way I will pay you whatever you spend on him." Sometimes the cost is considerable when we demonstrate compassion and love.

We may initially believe that love and concern for others will simply require our time, our energy, and our prayers, but there are times when it will cost us a great deal more. The Samaritan had his priorities in the right order. He was willing to give himself away, to give of his own financial resources, to help this injured man be healed and recuperated.

I've already discussed the relationship between our faith and material wealth, but the following are Biblical principles from R. Foster's book *Celebration of Discipline.* Remember that these are not some new laws for the Christian. The Gospel of Christ is about freedom, not slavery. These principles do incorporate many of the Biblical teachings about the use and possession of things and can give us insight as to how we should respond.

1. Give at least 10% of your income away. Let that percentage grow as your faith grows.
2. Reject anything which is producing an addiction in you. Get rid of any food or drink or possessions that you just cannot live without.
3. Develop a habit of giving things away. When you become very attached to some possession, give it to someone who needs it. De-accumulate. Masses of things that we do not need only complicate life. Most of us could get rid of half of our possessions without any serious sacrifice. Thoreau once said, "Simplify, simplify."
4. Refuse to be propagandized by the custodians of modern gadgetry. Most gadgets are built to break down and wear out. Foster describes this as buying things we don't need to impress people we don't like.
5. Learn to enjoy things without owning them. Owning things is an obsession in our culture. Share things with others.
6. Develop a deeper appreciation for God's creation. Get close to the earth, walk whenever you can, listen to the birds, marvel in the beauty of the colors—sky, sun, water, grass, flowers.
7. Look with healthy skepticism at all "buy now, pay later" schemes. They often serve to deepen your bondage. Use extreme caution for incurring debt, especially for that which decreases in value.
8. Reject anything that breeds the oppression of others. This is often complicated, and needs serious study. But we need a social consciousness as we purchase and consume.
9. Buy things for their usefulness rather than for their status.

10. Shun whatever distracts you from your main goal. Seek first the kingdom of God and his righteousness. Write a will that gives in death just as you have given in life. There are no U-hauls behind hearses these days.

We have no way of knowing if the Good Samaritan had adopted any or all of these ten principles listed above. But we can be sure that he was willing to use his money, perhaps at substantial risk to himself on behalf of another person, in fact, on behalf of a total stranger, one of another race and culture and background.

He was also willing to share his wealth in a situation where there was virtually no promise of any gain for himself. All that was present was the satisfaction of being able to help another human being, and that was enough for him. He knew about sacrificial giving, he knew the costly nature of compassion.

A story by Dr. Gerhard Frost from his book, *Bless My Growing,* gives us one more definition of compassion.

"It really wasn't much,
just a brown paper bag
with a piece of candy,
a few salted peanuts 'for now'
and a handful of cookies 'to take home'—
something to comfort a child
as she returned from the doctor's office.
But when she saw it
she exclaimed,
'Oh, grandma always remembers.'

It was the way she strung out
the 'al-ways'
that impressed me.
It reminded me that every life,
if it is to grow stong,
must have some 'always' people in it,